Crossroads of Life

Crossroads of Life

Making Tough Decisions Using Biblical Principles

Richard Godfrey

Edited by Joan Shock
Cover by Luke J. Godfrey
Foreword by Pastor Barry Palser

WESTBOW
PRESS
A DIVISION OF THOMAS NELSON

All Scripture quotations, unless otherwise indicated, are public domain, and taken from the Holy Bible, Authorized King James Version.
Amplified Bible: Je. 29:11; Ac. 9:5; 1 Pe. 5:23
Life Application Bible: Je. 29:11

WestBow Press books may be ordered through booksellers or by contacting:

WestBow Press
A Division of Thomas Nelson
1663 Liberty Drive
Bloomington, IN 47403
www.westbowpress.com
1-(866) 928-1240

ISBN: 978-1-4497-2460-3 (sc)
ISBN: 978-1-4497-2461-0 (hc)
ISBN: 978-1-4497-2459-7 (e)

Library of Congress Control Number: 2011914933

Printed in the United States of America

WestBow Press rev. date: 10-3-2011

CONTENTS

Endorsements and Testimonies

I've known the principles all my life, but it's good to have the process in written form for future reference.

—Joshua Little, student, Denver, CO

* * *

We learned and used these principles years ago. It's good to have them written down. Recommended reading for all ages.

—Mr. Jack Schultz, real estate broker, retired USAF, Ft. Wayne, IN

* * *

This book would be an excellent guide for group studies. It would benefit both the "Bible scholar" and the novice learner. The sharing of ideas and thoughts would be advantageous to both.

—JL, retired nurse, Oklahoma City, OK

* * *

Crossroads of Life is more than a book—it is a teaching manual, with so much in it, that can help those who have a basic knowledge of the Bible and wish to expand their knowledge of God. I highly recommend it.

—Jean Cox, retired facilitator, Aurora Public Schools, Aurora CO

* * *

We really loved this! We thought the language was especially good. It was as if we were sitting down and talking. We also liked the topics and how they flowed. There were questions we all ask from time to time . . . like "how did I get here?" The topics were thorough and Scripture inserted at just the right place. This is really excellent. We can see that the Lord used you in a mighty way! This is going to help a lot of people, including us. You did an awesome job! Wow! We're impressed!

—Gina Dickerson, hospitality executive, and Jon Dickerson, sales executive, Denver, CO

* * *

Richard Godfrey's book, *Crossroads of Life*, is a must read for anyone who has ever made a bad decision. The book encourages you to be more active and aggressive in your decision making instead of acquiescing to whatever is the easiest thing to do. The book has biblical principles for decision making that will help anyone make better decisions.

—Hugh Fells, associate pastor at Calvary Temple Church, Denver, CO

* * *

Some of us have so many options to choose from on a given circumstance that we become overwhelmed trying to make the right decision or just to make a decision period. Others see no alternative to very simple or extremely difficult situations. What is wrong with this picture?

During a conversation with Richard Godfrey about the difficulties families experience with their teens, he told me the reason that families are in the situations they are in, meaning precarious, was because they did not know how to make decisions. Richard then continued to share about a book he was writing to help people make decisions based on Biblical principles.

When I heard Richard talk about the steps people have to take to make sound decisions in their life based on the Bible, I could not be happier that there were others, Richard in this case, interested in empowering and helping people improve their own lives. It sounded similar to what I was offering to families through a program I had been offering at a public school, where I met Richard, by the way, only without the biblical references.

When Richard briefly explained to me some of the nine steps to making sound decisions, based on Bible principles, as he suggests in his *Crossroads of Life* book, I immediately suggested that he develop some kind of workshop where he could interactively present his material to the world. I thought it would be much more meaningful to put to practice what he was trying to convey abstractly, in other words, I would want as many people as possible, such as the families in the program I coordinated at that time, who would not necessarily be impelled to buy a book or who do not necessarily obtain their knowledge in a literary form, to actually benefit from the experience that a live presentation would provide.

The ideas in Richard's book would have greater impact on people. I thought if they could actually be walked through them. Real-life situations would be more effective and provide the opportunity for participants to rehearse the process and aptly apply it to their daily life; others would benefit and could be self-taught from the book.

Soon I found out that my advice can only be true if the person interacting with the content of the workshop, or the book for that matter, can only provide results if the person is willing to make him or herself vulnerable in the eyes of others in the workshop. Even more importantly, a person needs to be true to the self. Why do I say this? You will find a response a little later, but what you need to know first is that Richard took my advice and ran with it! He developed a workshop based on his book. He soon contacted me, informing me that he had a workshop ready and wanted to know if I would be interested in offering the secular version to families with school-aged children in my school district. A conversation with educational staff in charge of parent training took Richard nowhere in his pursuit, but hearing his discouragement, I promptly suggested he ask his church leaders to allow him to offer the workshop to their church community.

The *Crossroads of Life* workshops are now a part of history. Yes, Richard was able to offer his decision-making courses at his church and he invited me to participate. Remember that I said that it was easier said than done? What I meant by that is that going through the process and steps Richard suggests is easier said than done. As a participant, I first needed to identify a situation where I could apply the process. Identifying a situation was not the difficult part, since in life we are constantly faced with decisions. The difficulty resides in that if the situation is personal, more than likely it is going to involve discussions about those with whom the participants interact on a daily basis; family, friends, co-workers. Therefore, if these other people are not present to take part in the process, it really becomes uncomfortable, to say the least, to make them a part of the conversation. Then it would be talking about this other person or persons in their absence. For example, in a conversation about a spouse's desire to have the whole family attend church as a family (mom, dad, son, and daughter) when their spouse does not, inevitably the discussion brings that other person into the conversation. A lot of assumptions can be made about that person who is not present to respond.

In addition, there is ample opportunity for self-reflection and that can be "mind and soul drilling," so to speak. The latter not bad within itself, in fact, possibly the core intention of the whole process Richard developed.

In my case, attending Richard's decision-making course helped me do exactly that, dig into the depth of my own consciousness about both my individual responsibility for developing a closer relationship with God, and for how listening to God in making decisions regarding my interactions with others impacts, the outcome. In that sense, the decisions become more manageable. Nevertheless, I felt that had I been willingly to expose my thinking and doubts in the TOTAL sense with course participants, I might have been able to resolve my current dichotomy in life, not explicit herein.

But again, in reviewing the nine steps to decision-making, I not only as an educator, but also culturally need to reach out to "experts" and individuals with whom I feel more comfortable, disclosing my most profound thoughts on a particular personal situation. Therefore I will continue to strive for making decisions that are more difficult and those that manifest more hesitation, based on my ability to listen to God first, but also by following the well thought out steps offered in *Crossroads of Life* by Richard Godfrey.

I encourage you, the reader, to discover your own contradictions and beliefs about how to attain resolutions in every aspect of life and hope this book provides a great insight into that process. In case I did not clearly communicate what my position was while interacting with the material, let me restate that I found it very helpful and in line with my own beliefs. Utilizing the process for making decisions in a systematic manner led me to conclude that I do experience the proposed steps in my daily life. It also helped me to confirm that, when all the steps are in place, and most importantly, when the voice of God takes precedence, the results of the decisions are soothing to the mind, the body and the soul. Proof of a positive outcome, and in my opinion, that the decision was the appropriate one.

There is then no reason to remain overwhelmed by the plethora of options to choose from. Neither is it necessary to be overcome by simple or difficult situations. It is all a matter of knowing what we want, or what God wants us to do, and making the decision. It is all in the Bible.

—Flor Amaro, an urban educator with classroom instruction experience, extensive knowledge in site-based decision making and parental involvement in education in Denver, CO

"Enjoying the Fruit of Obedience to the Principles of
God's Word"
Richard Godfrey

"God is not into fire fighting, rather He is into fire
prevention. He would rather teach us to avoid
setting fires than to have to extinguish a four-alarm
fire in our personal lives."
Richard Godfrey

Foreword

Where we are today is a culmination of the decisions we have made in our lives. Before the end of our lives, we will have made thousands of decisions that not only affect our lives, but the lives of people with whom we have come into contact. You would think there would be a plethora of material to help us become better at decision making. But when was the last time you saw a book on this subject or heard a lecture on it?

Richard Godfrey has come up with some wonderful truths and insights to help us all in this critical part of our lives.

I recommend *Crossroads of Life—Making Tough Decisions Using Biblical Principles* for people of all ages. Not only will you become better at decision making after reading this book, but you will also be able to help others become better in this vital area of our lives. I would also recommend this book as a class course or small group material. The questions at the end of each chapter lend themselves well to a variety of small group formats.

I am also thankful to Richard Godfrey for giving us fresh insight into one of the most important aspects of our lives—decisions. May your decision making never be the same after reading this life-changing book.

Barry Palser
Senior pastor of Calvary Temple, Denver, Colorado

Acknowledgments

God will often give a person a task that he is not prepared for, but He will supply all that is necessary to accomplish the task. Moses comes to mind, having absolutely no skills. God gave him the daunting task of building the tabernacle in the wilderness. Then he provided skilled craftsmen and women to bond together, each one with their several skills, to accomplish the task of building the tabernacle. Similarly, I have no writing skills, save what the Master wrings from me. I, therefore, like Moses, have had to use the expertise of others more skilled in writing than I.

There have been so many who have encouraged and helped me as the *Crossroads of Life* manuscript progressed to what it is today.

It is one thing to do something you are familiar with and have the skills to accomplish and quite another to attempt something about which you have absolutely no clue. It is the latter which teaches patience and perseverance like no other task can accomplish.

First, I give honor to my Lord and Savior, Jesus Christ, for laying *Crossroads* on my heart. Throughout the entire process I've learned to wait on him for guidance and inspiration. It is He who has kept me all along the way. I give him the highest praise and a heartfelt thank you for keeping me along the way, and especially for sending the right person at the right time to assist in this endeavor. He alone knows that I am not a writer. Therefore, it is proof positive that God has a sense of humor.

Second, I thank my beloved wife and companion, Diane, for standing beside me through thick and thin with love, devotion, and prayers.

To my son, Luke, for his computer expertise and patient understanding of my computer challenges, as well as for the beautiful cover design.

To my eldest son, Byron, for his love, devotion, encouragement, and advice.

A special thanks goes to Senior Pastor Barry Palser, Calvary Temple, Denver, for trusting and believing in me to teach the *Crossroads of Life* series for fourteen weeks at Calvary Temple.

Also to Pastor Barry's executive secretaries, Kate Linde and Deana Mills, for their gracious and tireless help in numerous areas as the manuscript progressed. Their hard work and dedication made the teaching series a tremendous success.

Numerous others gave support and insightful help along the way: Craig Chambron, Jean Cox, Flor Amora, Deanne Holmes, and Ann Schultz.

To the willing, yet unwary, participants in the *Crossroads of Life* series, I give special thanks of gratitude for allowing me to expound on the unchartered waters of the very rough draft. Your patience and participation was inspiring.

To a junior and senior high school classmate, whom I'd never met, but who, when she got wind of the project, unselfishly volunteered to edit my labor of love: thank you.

Love in Christ,
Richard Godfrey

Introduction

How to Use This Book

I wrote this book primarily because I was always a terrible decision maker and had the desire and need to improve dramatically in this important area of life. Secondly, it was recommended by a doctor as treatment for a mild traumatic brain injury suffered in a car and semi-tractor accident. Thirdly, it was a God given mandate to help others who suffer from lack of good decision-making skills.

I wish people could simply turn to a specific page in a book and find the answer to their selective problem. However, that is an impossible endeavor, as details of similar problems may differ widely.

Crossroads of Life is intended to give the reader the necessary tools to make better choices; not to make decisions for them.

1. *Crossroads of Life* is designed for group study and discussion. One person may serve as a moderator, rather than lecturer. I have discovered that the open discussion model works more efficiently and effectively. However, an individual may still experience success without the benefit of group study.

2. Find the appropriate principle(s) applicable to your problem in the "Starter Concordance of Biblical Principles." (Note there are many more principles in God's word than

I have recorded in these pages or index; therefore, the readers are encouraged to add to the index as needed.) The principle may or may not identify the consequence, whether good or bad.

3. Lesson 3 outlines the biblical process of decision making. Simply follow the process. (Note: some decisions may not require a complete process. The individual problem will identify which steps to take.)

4. The principles are suitable for teaching all ages about correct decision making. Even if you have a track record of making bad decisions, this book will assist you in changing your bad patterns. Parents may also find this a useful tool in teaching their children how to make good decisions.

5. At the end of each chapter is a series of questions entitled: "Faith Building Practice and Review," designed to help you retain what you have read and to build your faith at the same time. Prayerfully review each lesson and answer each question.

6. The principles will work even if you are not a believer in Jesus Christ. They will work no matter what your religion,. the reason being that the same God who established universal laws of morality and ethics created everyone. *Crossroads of Life* lends itself to adaptability as an instrument for teaching decision making in the home or in churches.

7. *Crossroads of Life* will also help the reader learn to:

- study and understand the Scriptures
- understand the relevancy of Scriptures to contemporary life
- build the reader's faith by trusting God's Word on a whole new level

Abbreviations
The Books of the Old Testament

Genesis	Gen.	Ecclesiastes	Eccl.
Exodus	.Ex	The Song of Solomon	Song
Leviticus	Lev.	Isaiah	Isa.
Numbers	Num.	Jeremiah	Jer.
Deuteronomy	Deut.	Lamentations	Lam.
Joshua	Josh.	Ezekiel	Ezek.
Judges	Judg.	Daniel	Dan.
Ruth	Ruth	Hosea	Hos.
1 Samuel	1 Sam.	Joel	Joel
2 Samuel	2 Sam.	Amos	Amos
1 Kings	1 Kings	Obadiah	Obad.
2 Kings	2 Kings	Jonah	Jonah
1 Chronicles	1Chron.	Micah	Mic.
2 Chronicles	2 Chron.	Nahum	Nah.
Ezra	Ezra	Habakkuk	Hab.
Nehemiah	Neh.	Zephaniah	Zeph.
Esther	Est.	Haggai	Hag.
Job	Job	Zechariah	Zech.
Psalms	Ps.	Malachi	Mal.
Proverbs	Prov.		

The Books of the New Testament

Matthew	Matt.	1Timothy	1Tim.
Mark	Mark	2Timothy	2Tim.
Luke	Luke	Titus	Tit.
John	John	Philemon	Phm.
The Acts	Acts.	Hebrews	Heb.
Romans	Rom.	James	James
1 Corinthians	1Cor.	1Peter	1Peter
2 Corinthians	2Cor.	2Peter	2Peter
Galatians	Gal.	1 John	1John

Lesson 1

Introductory Lesson

Psalm 25:5 "Lead me in the truth and teach me: for thou art the God of my salvation; on thee do I wait all the day."

Jer. 29:11 "For I know the thoughts that I think toward you, saith the Lord, thoughts of peace, and not of evil, to give you an expected end" (Life Application Bible).

Decisions, decisions! Everyday life is full of choices that demand our attention.

- Cereal or eggs? Bacon? Oatmeal?
- Cash, check, debit, or credit?
- Sleep in, rise early, or be on time?
- What time should I eat?
- Drive, walk, carpool, or cab? How about the bus?
- Should I go to college? If so, which one?
- A college or university? Community college?
- What should I major in? What should I minor in?
- What do I want to be when I grow up?
- Should I work or not?
- Whom should I marry and why?

- Divorce or reconciliation?
- Children or none? How many?
- What church should I/we attend? Which denomination?

These and countless other choices bombard each of us every day. Some solutions are easier than others. Some require more thought and consideration. Some may have more far-reaching consequences than others, such as which car to buy, whether to change jobs and move across town or out of state, or whom to marry.

The simple ones we seem to handle rather easily, almost without thinking. However, it's the more difficult ones that trouble us the most. Some decisions are quite painful and arduous to make and have the potential to send us into an emotional tailspin, which, if not checked, can and will lead to a physical, mental, and spiritual breakdown.

> "Making decisions is very scary for me. I wish it were easier." —Anonymous

> "I am very bad at making decisions. It seems like everything always turns out bad for me. My decision making is atrocious!" —Chuck, Colorado Springs, CO

Therefore, it is of utmost importance to remember the following:

> Isa. 26:3-4 "God will keep him in perfect peace whose mind is stayed on Him: because he trusts in thee. Trust in the Lord for ever: for in Jehovah is everlasting strength."

Remember, it is the one who keeps his mind on the Lord, not on his problems, who receives peace.

> Matt. 6:33-34 "But seek ye first the kingdom of God, and his righteousness; and all these things shall be added

unto you. Take therefore no thought for the morrow: for the morrow shall take thought of the things of it. Sufficient unto the day is the evil thereof."

1 Peter 5:6 "Humble yourselves therefore under the mighty hand of God, that He may exalt you in due time: Casting all your care upon Him: for He cares for you."

The way we humble ourselves before God is to cast, throw, or give to Him all our troubles, believing Him and trusting Him while waiting patiently and obediently for Him.

> "Jesus is our burden bearer. Only He is able to shoulder all our cares and woes."
> —Author unknown

Making tough decisions does not exempt us from trusting Him (which is not easy to do), as we are so used to operating in the flesh and doing things ourselves, often giving precious little thought to honestly trusting Him. As a result, we end up giving lip service only, with our heart far from Him, and we take Him and our "faith" for granted.

Matt. 11:28-30 "Come unto me, all you who labor and are heavy laden or weighted down with care, and I will give you rest. Take my yoke upon you, and learn of me; for I am meek and lowly in heart: and you shall find rest unto your souls. For my yoke is easy and my burden is light."

How Did I Get Here?

We are where we are today because of the decisions we made yesterday. Therefore, wherever we are tomorrow will depend on the decisions we make today. Granted, we may try to shift the blame to someone or something else rather than owning up to our own decisions, but the ultimate decision is ours and ours alone. Therefore, the consequences belong to us as well.

Since the beginning of time, God has given man what we call free will. That is, we are free to make decisions as we choose—but not without consequences. Free will may also be called "individual will." Some might even refer to it as God's "permissive will."

Adam and Eve were given a choice—namely, that they could eat of everything except the tree of knowledge of good and evil. That is God's sovereign will. And that's why we are where we are today. Adam chose, we choose. It's as simple as that!

Moses put forth a choice to the children of Israel either to serve the Lord God and be blessed or to choose other gods and be cursed. Later, Elijah the prophet gave the same choice to the wayward children of Israel. See 1Kings 18:21: "How long halt ye between two opinions? If the Lord be God, follow him: but if Baal, then follow Him."

Isn't it curious that the people were silent following the challenge, "answering him not a word"?

Every decision has consequences, either good or bad. There is no such thing as a neutral choice or decision that is devoid of consequences. If the decision is wrong, the outcome is cursed and cannot be blessed.

The question therefore becomes "How can I make good decisions?" Unfortunately, many of us fail in this crucial area, I suspect, because:

1. No one ever taught us how to make good decisions at home, in the church, or in society itself. Therefore, we followed the role models in our lives, good or bad.
2. We know how to make good decisions but choose to ignore the principles of good decision making.

The very idea of asking for God's direction is foreign to us, as it requires waiting for and listening to God's voice, which is contrary to the flesh (i.e., way too slow). Therefore, it is easier and simpler to leave God out and proceed in the flesh and then blame God later when we are unsuccessful or have a less-than-desirable outcome. With few exceptions, learning how to hear God's voice is simply not taught in churches today, for whatever reason. Read lesson 3 on hearing God's voice.

It is a fact of life that absolutely no one is right *all* the time, just as no one is ever wrong *all* the time!

Author's Note: If we could make just 50 percent of our decisions correctly, we would be very successful. If that's true, just think how successful we would be if *all* our decisions were correct.

Our prisons are full of those who have made wrong and very bad decisions. Marriages fail because of bad choices; jobs are lost due to poor judgment. Financial decisions, bankruptcy, and enormous debt are the direct result of poor decision making. Divorces, marital discord, and the birth of children out of wedlock are also the result of poor decisions.

On and on they go! Simply stated, decisions are a cause-and-effect phenomenon. The biblical term is "sowing and reaping."

If you are wondering why you are where you are in any of life's situations, simply look at where you are now and backtrack your steps; you will realize how the choices you made got you where you are.

Because only God knows the future, only God is able to make good decisions 100 percent of the time! However, God has given some guidelines or principles that will make us prosperous and successful if studied and applied.

Although I realize there are individuals who are classified as type-A personalities with the ability or gift of almost instantaneous, shoot-from-the-hip decisiveness, I suspect they may be able to use some of the thoughts I share. Even these persons do not make *all* their decisions without counsel from trusted sources.

Crossroads of Life was written from personal need and experience. Like many others, I was never taught *how* to make decisions. Rather, my choices were mostly made for me.

For example:

- I was told not to marry so and so, but not how to choose or select my life-long partner or what to look for when considering one. Consequently, I made two very wrong marital decisions, both of which ended in disaster.
- I was told not to purchase this car or that car, but not how to compare automobiles, amenities, gas mileage, warranties, and so on.
- My place of worship was predetermined from youth, which is not necessarily bad; however, I was not instructed on why or how to choose one church or denomination over the other. I was told what faith was the correct one. I was not instructed on how to either choose a different "correct faith" or maintain the faith I had. I was simply to assume that the church I had attended all the days of my youth was the correct one!
- I was told not to associate with this person or that person or to establish friendships with certain people. However, I was never taught how to select friends and associates that were "good" and "acceptable."
- I was told, concerning money, "not to let it burn a hole in my pocket" and "not to spend it all in one place." However, I was never taught sound financial principles on saving, investing, comparison shopping, etc.

One has only to pick up the local newspaper and read about some of the bad decisions people have made to see the consequences they suffer as a result. Not only do they make a ruin of their own reputations and lives, but their bad decisions have a trickle-down effect, touching and forever changing the lives of their immediate family, friends, co-workers, etc. For example, the act of murder of one person creates a child without a parent, grandchildren without a grandparent, and a widow. Emotional tidal waves are created by a single act of careless behavior!

You can read about federal judges asking their "personal" prostitutes to lie about their relationships. Celebrities from the entertainment and sports world are getting caught for illegal drug use and/or possession, or speeding, or driving under the influence of alcohol. Even prominent media people are being exposed for their improper decisions. Maybe they misrepresent the facts on a story they are covering, or maybe their affair of long ago has come to light. Men and women alike are judged in trial before their peers and convicted of heinous crimes. Political leaders from the top down are exposed for wrongdoing! Recently, financial "experts" have been investigated for violating sound business and financial principles. All are guilty of making wrong, hurtful decisions.

Principle: Luke12:2-3 "For there is nothing covered, that shall not be revealed; neither hid, that it shall not be known. Therefore whatsoever ye have spoken in darkness shall be heard in the light; and that which ye have spoken in the ear in closets shall be proclaimed upon the housetops."

That simply means that no matter what we do or say in private, sooner or later it will be published openly, in one form or another. Simply read the daily newspaper. With Jesus, there are no secrets. We live in the presence of an all knowing God.

Principle: Psalm139:1-2 "O Lord, thou hast searched me, and known me. Thou knowest mine downsitting and mine uprising, thou understandeth my thought afar off."

Continue to read through verse 13 and you will discover that the God we serve knows all about us, even our thoughts before we can utter them. Therefore, while it is nice to be recognized in this life, it is far better to be rewarded by God in His timing.

On the other hand, to be fair, there are a relatively few cases of a person's good decisions being publicized. For instance, a person may be acknowledged for bravery for rescuing a drowning person or animal, or for assisting authorities in the apprehension and conviction of a wrong doer. What kind of notoriety are you willing to live with? Are you willing to practice "random acts of kindness" and receive no notoriety?

My dad used to tell me, "If you get into trouble, and it's your fault, you can sit there in jail. But if you are innocent, I'll fight for you!" And he meant every word of it! Because of his philosophy, I rarely got into trouble and never into real serious trouble. I was too scared! Praise the Lord! However, if I did get in trouble in school, no matter how minor, I always caught it when Dad got home. In those days the schools kept the parents informed and I learned to keep my nose as clean as possible.

Definition of Prosperity and Success:

"Enjoying the fruit of obedience to the principles of God's Word."—Richard Godfrey

I believe that one may be prosperous and successful in ways other than material wealth. For example, by adhering to biblical principles, your secular relationships, as well as those within the church, in business, marriage, child rearing, etc., may be successful and prosperous. They may or may not include an increase in material wealth.

God's Word

The following principles assure us of prosperity and success, if we obey them.

1. Principle: Genesis 2:17 "But of the tree of the knowledge of good and evil, thou shalt not eat of it: for in the day that thou eatest thereof thou shall surely die."
   In other words, obedience to God's Word assures prosperity and success manifested by life as opposed to death.
2. Principle: Joshua 1:6-8 " . . . Observe to do all according to the law . . . turn not to the right or left . . .

meditate day and night . . . prosper whithersoever thou goest."

3. Principle: Isaiah 1:19-20 "If ye be willing and obedient, ye shall eat the good of the land: but if ye refuse and rebel ye shall be devoured with the sword: for the mouth of the Lord hath spoken it."

4. Principle: Jeremiah 29:11 "For I know the thoughts that I think toward you, saith the Lord, thoughts of peace, and not evil, to give you an expected end."

   "For I know the plans I have for you, plans of welfare and not evil, to give you a future and a hope." Amplified Bible

Some may argue that the Old Testament was written specifically for the children of Israel and not for the New Testament church. My response is: Why should God desire some of his children to prosper and be successful and not others? Through studies of the Scriptures, it is revealed that God really does want us all to prosper and succeed in all areas of life. Compare: Ex. 19:5, Deut. 14:2, Deut. 26:18, Psalm 135:4, Eccl 2:8, with Tit. 2:14 and 2 Peter 2:9.

While the Old Testament was written to the children of Israel, the principles for their successes are nonetheless applicable to the church today and applicable to all mankind. Consider the prospect that if the secular community were to obey God's Word, it would also be very successful and prosperous. In many ways, the secular community may appear more prosperous and successful than believers in the church. In other ways, the secular community falls short, simply because it follows some biblical principles, either intentionally or unintentionally.

Why? The same God who created moral and ethical principles, also created the same principles for all mankind. There are not two different standards—one for nonbelievers and one for believers.

For example, I know personally of thriving marriages, people in unsaved (secular) relationships, who unknowingly apply the principles of love without ever having studied or read the Bible.

Principle: Romans 2:14-15 "For when the gentiles, which have not known the law, do by nature the things contained in the law, these having not the law, are a law unto themselves: which shew the work of the law written in their hearts, their conscience also bearing witness, and their thoughts the meanwhile accusing or else excusing one another."

According to the above verse, even a nonbeliever knows adultery is wrong. It is a universal principal of morality and ethics. Therefore, many will refuse to commit adultery, their conscience bearing witness. That person or relationship is blessed!

The passage clearly indicates that God's laws or principles of morality and ethics are indeed universal and applicable to the secular society as well as the church.

This Scripture in Rom. 2:14-15 is not a reference to just the Ten Commandments. Rather, it includes the entire book of the Law of Moses, which encompasses the laws of morality and ethics, which some call the moral law or will, as well as the sovereign will of God.

The book of Proverbs was written to give "instruction of wisdom, justice, and judgment, and equity" (Prov. 1:1-6). It provides godly wisdom and knowledge for daily life to assist in the prosperity, success, and well-being of God's people in literally every arena of life: financial, relationships, et cetera. It provides contrasts between the way of the wicked versus the way of the righteous. It was, for the most part, written by a loving father, Solomon, to his beloved children, to instruct them on how to be successful and to prosper by choosing between right and wrong.

Right living very often leads to some measure of "prosperity," but is not an absolute guarantee, depending on one's definition of prosperity. If you choose the definition stated above (enjoying the fruit of obedience to the principles of God's Word), then right living does, in fact, bring prosperity.

For example, my wife, Diane, and I are faithful in giving our tithes and offerings. As a result, our resources have never "dried up." We live in a comfortable home. The bills we do have are paid because God is faithful to His Word and because we live by the biblical principles of tithes and offerings. As I was writing this, a friend called to ask if we could help provide school uniforms for some kids, and we volunteered with haste. That, to us, is success and prosperity! When we are faithful and punctual at our places of employment, we are successful every payday. Conversely, if we neglect our work ethic, we experience a "curse" which is the predetermined consequence, namely unemployment. The choice is ours!

Principle: Proverbs 1:20-33 outlines the results for hearing and disobeying or rejecting wisdom. "I will not answer . . . I will laugh and mock at your calamity."

It is evident from Scripture that God not only desires for us to be prosperous and successful, but also that He has given us directions and instructions to be prosperous and successful. Therefore, true success and prosperity are not only obtained, but also defined in God's terms, and not ours. The solution then rests with each of us as believers to search out and obey the Word.

I am not proposing a "cause and effect" relationship between God and man. Rather, by adhering to divine principles, we can avert unnecessary or predetermined calamity and experience a predetermined "blessing" of success and prosperity.

Faith Building Practice and Review

1. List three ways you are blessed.

2. List three ways you are cursed.

3. Wouldn't you rather be blessed than cursed? Why?

4. Explain the difference between a blessing and a curse.

5. Have you given much thought to the fact that your ability to make good biblical decisions may determine your future, just as it has your past?

6. Prayerfully list three areas of your life in which you seem to make the same bad decisions over and over.

7. For each of the above listed areas, prayerfully find at least four biblical principles that will guide you to make a better decision next time.

8. Ask God to give you wisdom to reverse the way you've been making bad decisions.

Notes

Notes

Lesson 2

Various Methods of Decision-Making

The methods listed here give realization to the many methods people have used throughout the ages to make decisions. It is not an exhaustive list, but contains most of the major and popular methods. They stand in stark contrast to the biblical process. Perhaps you will relate to one or more of them.

Astrology and stargazing: attempts to make decisions based upon the alignment of the stars, and *attempt* to place people into so-called "personality types" according to the signs of the zodiac. I don't know about you, but I'm glad my life doesn't depend on whether or not my stars are lined up correctly! You can thank your lucky stars for that!

Divination: the process, or activity, of trying to foretell the future, or discovering hidden knowledge, by means other than seeking the Lord God Jehovah (See Deut. 18:10-12). Divination methods include tea leaves, horoscopes, astrology and stargazing.

Horoscope consultation: Published in newspapers and tabloids across the country and the world, horoscopes can mislead and seduce people into mindlessly and faithfully following questionable assertions. Horoscopes are really nothing to laugh at, as they can lead unwary individuals into damnable situations. The irony is that those who profit from them, temporarily at least, are the persons who write them. Many supposedly smart and intellectual individuals follow their pernicious advice as well.

Occultism: includes palm and tarot card readings, séances, familiar spirits, and Ouija boards. The list goes on and on.

Principle: Deuteronomy 18:10-12 "When you come into the land which the LORD thy God gives you, thou shall not learn to do after the abominations of those nations. There shall not be found among you any one that makes his son or daughter to pass through the fire or that uses divination, or an observer of times, or enchanter, or a witch, or a charmer or a consultant with familiar spirits, or a wizard, or a necromancer. For all that do these things are an abomination to the LORD: and because of these abominations the LORD thy God doth drive them out from before you."

The question remains: Why are the above practices forbidden by God? The answer is simply because they are demonic or subversive in nature and lead people away from serving and loving the Creator. They begin, ever so slowly, to corrupt the character of the person, which leads to the destruction of the faith that is necessary to maintain a relationship with the Lord, thus opening the door to worship and serve other gods.

When we were in the world, we lived according to the worldly ways of living, including making decisions. However, after we became children of God, we needed to learn new and godly methods.

Idolaters attempt to manipulate the Lord for their own purposes. Persons of faith know this is useless, and teach themselves to wait on Him for their provision, instead of trying to "make" Him provide for their needs.

God simply does not take it lightly when we use the above practices. Besides being extremely ambiguous and unreliable, horoscopes also fall under the category of divination. Remember King Saul in 1Sam. 28:6-20, when he sought counsel from the witch of Endor who had a familiar spirit? He wanted her to raise Samuel up from the dead for advice. The result of his disobedience was that God tore (signifying violence) the kingdom from Saul and his posterity, and delivered him and his sons into the hands of the Philistines (their enemies) for death.

Biblical roulette: the equivalent practice of "pin-the-tail-on-the-donkey," where someone closes their eyes, opens the Bible, puts a finger on a verse, opens their eyes and assumes it for divine direction. Another variation is when a verse "pops out" or "illuminates" when a reader scans it and it is taken for divine revelation and/or direction.

Casting lots: "The use of the lot, as a mode of settling disputed questions, is very ancient, and was practiced by most ancient nations. It was resorted to in reference to almost all the varied affairs of life. Magistrates and priests were appointed by it, and the land of conquered enemies was distributed by its means.

We have no information given in Scripture concerning the mode by which lots were cast. Among the Latins, especially where several parties were concerned, little counters of wood, or some other light material, were put into a jar (called *sitella*) with a neck so narrow that only one could come out at a time. After the jar had been filled with water and the contents shaken, the lots were determined by the order in which the bits of wood, representing the several parties, came out of the water."[1]

In Acts 1:15-26, the disciples were faced with the challenge of selecting one man to replace Judas Iscariot (who had hung himself after betraying Jesus). After determining the qualifications, they selected two men and relied on the old-fashioned method of casting lots to choose who should replace Judas. Casting lots was an Old Testament practice mentioned numerous times in the scriptures. Aaron used it in Le.16:8 to determine which goat should be slain for the Lord and which should be the scapegoat, a type of Christ and Barabbas.

---

[1] *Bible Manners and Customs* by James M. Freeman, pg. 237, 463—The Lot, para.1, copyright 1972, copied by permission.

Principle: Proverbs16:33 "The lot causes contentions to cease, and parts between the mighty." Prov. 18:18 "The lot is cast into the lap, but the whole disposing thereof is of the Lord."

In other words, God sanctions the casting of lots. Not only that, but He is also in divine control of it, as absolutely nothing takes God by surprise. It is, therefore, an acceptable manner to resolve or decide issues where more than one person is involved.

Coin toss: Some sports, such as football, use this method to determine which team receives first and even which end zone will be defended.

Column method: A line is drawn down the middle of a sheet of paper and "For" is placed in one column, and "Against" in the other. As many "for" or "against" reasons as possible are listed in the each column and tallied. The column with the most reasons wins. Not always a bad way to make a decision. It can aid in clarifying the situation so the person can see what needs to be done, or where the problem areas lie.

Dictatorship: a one-person method. For example, Adolph Hitler made the decisions and established tyranny to implement his ways.

Follow the leader: From time to time I hear of someone making a decision simply because a friend or friends made the same decision. They simply followed out of a need for acceptance or as a path of least resistance. In the days of our childhood it was very popular.

Godly counsel: The book of Proverbs admonishes us to seek the counsel of not one, but several, godly persons. But be wary of the counselors you seek. Make sure they are persons of God with practical experience, who can think on their own and who will submit controversy when appropriate. The last thing you want is a "yes man" for your counsel. You need controversy to insure that all bases are covered, if possible. People who "rubber-stamp" your decisions are careless and dangerous. Sometimes they will avoid dissention for the sake of remaining in good standing with you. Likewise, you don't want someone who consistently opposes everything. Either can happen with a board of directors in both secular and church entities.

He or she loves me, or loves me not: This method involves pulling off the petals of a flower. When you run out of petals with an undesirable conclusion, you simply start all over with another flower. Most often, this is used when looking for a mate or employment. This method is used over and over again until we get the answer we want. Very seldom does it work out, and if, by chance, it does, the flower gets the praise and glory, not the Creator! Hmm! The practice was popular in the days of our youth. However, hopefully it is discarded before disastrous consequences occur.

Whatever happened to becoming the best person you could be, or looking for the best person as a marriage partner, or updating your resume, or better yet, learning new skills to make yourself more valuable?

By all means, enjoy the beauty and fragrance of the flowers, but please don't use them to make decisions. That is, unless you're willing to live by the consequences.

Peace: A common teaching is that you experience peace when you're in the will of God. However, Jonah was fast asleep ("at peace") in the ship during the storm, but he was out of God's will by going to Joppa. I find this to be somewhat normal, as quite often a decision will be made that gives at least a temporary peace. After a while, though, we, like Jonah, become convicted and our peace is interrupted, ushering in unrest.

It appears, although somewhat subjectively, that David experienced the same temporary peace in his episode with Bathsheba and the subsequent cover-up of Uriah's murder, and later in his grief when confronted by Nathan the prophet. Peace in and of itself is not an all-out, reliable indicator of a good decision.

Let's explore this idea of peace a bit more. I believe in most instances that peace is essential; however, peace will not, and cannot, be attained without first going through the process of prudent decision making.

Neither David nor Jonah had a true, lasting peace, as theirs was not prudent decision making. They simply decided without counsel, either from godly men or the Scriptures, to satisfy their own lusts. That is why they were emotionally disturbed later when discovered.

Theocracy: (1) A form of government in which God or a deity is recognized as the supreme civil ruler, (2) A system of government by priests claiming a divine commission.[2]

Moses was God's spokesman for the children of Israel during the exodus from Egypt and subsequent sojourn of forty years in the wilderness. Moses received his directives directly from the Lord God.

Urim and Thummim: Review the passage in 1Sam. 30:1-8. When David and his men returned to Ziklag after volunteering for battle in alliance with the Philistines, they discovered the Amalekites had burned the city and had taken their women captive. David encouraged himself in the Lord, and sought direction with the Urim and Thummim, which was carried in the ephod of the priest, and received his answer. If that's divination, we need to be extremely careful! The Urim and Thummim was God's approved method for the priests to seek his guidance. David had peace in this decision to pursue the Amalekites with God's directive. In the Old Testament, the Urim means, "light" and Thummim means "perfections" or "perfections of truth."

Jesus declared himself to be "the way, the truth and the light" (John 4:6.). Therefore, He is our Urim and Thummim today! David was seeking God's perfect will and way in pursuing the Amakelites. We can do that today.

---

[2]   Random House Dictionary of the English Language (1968), 1362

Principle: Psalm119:105 "thy word is a lamp unto my feet [showing where I am] and a light unto my path" [showing and giving direction of where to go].

Life begins anew at salvation, when we trust Christ's finished work on Calvary, which means that we need to learn to trust God's word to direct our every path. And that requires teaching.

Voting: Voting is another avenue for making decisions. In democratic societies, voting is the accepted norm for making decisions, as well as for the election of officials. It is a formal expression of a personal opinion. Not only that, but the Bible states that the outcome of the vote is the Lord's. In other words, God sanctions the vote, and by so doing, we have set up His person at the right time. So don't be angry when your candidate loses. God's person still won, regardless of which party they are with. Contrary to popular, false belief, God is not Republican, Democrat, Liberal, Independent, nor a member of any other political party!

Isn't it curious that all of Israel's victories in battle with its enemies were won by consulting the Commander-in-Chief (Jehovah), and all their defeats were directly related to not seeking His counsel? Look at Joshua, at the famous battle of Jericho (Josh. 1:1-27), or at Gideon's battle against the Philistines (Judg. 7:1-25), when the Israelites were heavily out-numbered.

By the way, don't be surprised if God gives you counsel that defies human logic. I wonder what Joshua and Gideon's captains thought when told of the battle plans. (Just make sure it is God who gives you the instructions.) See lesson 4: "Hearing God's Voice."

If it were true in ancient Israel that the people needed Godly counsel, why wouldn't it be true for you and me today? Study those "righteous people" who lived before Moses. To whom do they owe the success of their victories? For example, did Noah take it upon himself to build a boat? No, he followed explicit instructions from the Lord God. Was he successful? Yes, for his family was saved from the flood to repopulate the earth. Abraham left his homeland, country, kinfolk and his father's house to seek a land that God had promised him. He became the father, not only of Israel, but also of the faithful throughout succeeding generations, and even today. How much more should we seek the counsel of the Living God?

Strictly speaking, God wants us to prosper and be successful. He cannot, and will not, allow us to prosper when we continually and wantonly make decisions in the flesh! Therefore, isn't it wiser to seek Godly methods for making decisions?

Faith Building Practice and Review

1. How many different ways to make decisions are listed?

2. List all the ways that you have tried recently.

3. Now explain the general outcome of using your techniques.

4. Have you ever used occult methods to make decisions?

5. Are you still involved in the occult? Explain.

6. Why are occult practices so dangerous?

7. Is Jesus your Urim and Thummim? If not, why not?

Notes

Notes

Lesson 3

Nine Step Biblical Process of Decision-Making

Good decision-making is about acknowledging God, getting His direction and becoming educated on the subject at hand. That education involves asking critical questions which may affect the outcome of the decision, either positively or negatively. The word of God gives many examples of decisions with positive and negative consequences.

The family is, in one sense, a business not unlike any other business, whether it is in the private sector or government, and as such, needs to operate like a business. All businesses, whether private, church, or governmental, have the responsibility to make rational decisions on a daily basis. Therefore, in order to survive, they must have a process for making those decisions. Because no individual has the corner on the market for making decisions, the decisions are usually made by a group of two or more people, depending on the size of the business.

The future of every family, business, or government rests on the decisions made daily. Those decisions made today, whether good or bad, will often impact the entity for generations to come. For singles or single parents, it is wise to seek out mature, trusted friends and relatives to assist them in the decision-making process.

The Process

1. Acknowledge the Lord. Prov. 3:5-6: "Trust in the Lord with all thine heart; and lean not unto thine own understanding. In all thy ways acknowledge him, and he shall direct thy paths."
    To acknowledge the Lord means much more than praying the simple prayer of "Lord help me" as I do this or that. The phrase "in all thy ways" implies that we pray and seek God's directives each and every step, until the final decision is made, through prayer and discovering the biblical principles applicable to the situation.

2. Accurately identify and clarify the problem or concern. If you don't clarify the problem or concern, then all the work and effort you put into the solution will be wasted. For example, you may think getting a second job will solve your financial woes. However, careful examination of God's Word may reveal that you are violating financial principals. You may also discover that all you really need is to learn how to better manage your money. You may indeed get another job or pay raise, but if you haven't applied God's financial principles and learned how to better manage your money, then you have in effect multiplied your problems instead of solved them. So, without first identifying the problem and applying God's principles, you simply cannot proceed to the next step with good results.
    God's Word will point you in the direction you need to go.

3. Determine what information is needed to solve the problem. This involves research and looking for relevant information. For example, if you are going on a vacation to Germany, you will first need to check travel and accommodations including airfare, hotel and rental car fares.

4. Analyze the information. Prov. 3:6b: "lean not unto thine own understanding";
Principle: Proverbs 3:13: "Happy is the man that findeth wisdom, and the man that getteth understanding."

Analyze all the information you acquire from several airlines, cruise lines, hotels, and car rental businesses, compare prices, amenities etc., and then seek to understand the information by reading the fine print and asking questions of concern. Prov. 2:2b: "apply thine heart to understanding." That is getting God's perspective of the particular situation.

5. Seek wisdom, information and advice from others. Prov. 1:20-33: Check with friends and relatives who've been to Germany to discover whether or not they got better deals.

Author's Note: If married, both husband and wife should have equal input in all decisions. If not, one or the other may feel devalued, not respected, and/or not important enough. Then one could be viewed as a dictator or manipulator. It is wise to have equal input from both parties, as one may see something the other may miss. Both perspectives are vital.

6. Determine which (if any) Biblical principles might be violated, and identify potential consequences (Prov. 1:7, 24). If you're conducting a business deal, make certain you are dealing with persons who are honest and have integrity. If their ideas or plans sound a bit shady, they probably are! Check out all material information. In other words, check out the potential end results, whether good or bad. If you have violated even one principle, you will pay the price and suffer the penalty. Remember, every decision has consequences, be they good or bad. The question remains: "Can you live with the results?"

7. Discard irrelevant information. Perhaps some of the information on your "big business deal" is unnecessary and immaterial. Discard it so you aren't encumbered or confused with it later.

8. Determine the best solution. There may very well be several seemingly good solutions to your problem. With proper counsel, wisdom, and information from others, you will arrive at the best solution.

9. Implement the solution. Don't dawdle! If you've done your homework and research, and have reached an acceptable conclusion, by all means do it!

"I can do all my research, seek advice, and make comparisons, purchase the product and take it home, only to change my mind later and either return it or exchange it. It seems like every decision is this way, whether it be big or small!" Karen, Denver, CO.

Seek Wise Counsel

Principle: Seek wise counsel. Proverbs11:14b "But in the multitude of counselors there is safety."

Wisdom, Where Is It?

Principle: read Proverbs1:20-23

Two Kinds of Wisdom

Earthly wisdom engenders: James3:14-16

- Bitterness and envy
- Strife
- Confusion
- Evil work: this one is wide open, encompassing lying, cheating, bearing false witness, jealousy etc.

- That which is sensual in nature: that is, not spiritual, strictly carnal. (Sensual meaning it is operating from the flesh.)
- That which is devilish in nature: appealing to the sensual and emotional side of us.
- The person from whom you seek wisdom must first prove him or herself, showing a lifestyle of integrity and good works, with meekness. In other words, they must have demonstrated their life and earned a good reputation with many others.

The products of wisdom from above are: James 3:17-18

- Meekness: synonymous with being humble, patient or even submissive and still self-confident.
- Purity: not mixed with evil intentions.
- Peaceableness and gentleness: not giving occasion for the emotional side to be aroused within you.
- Ability to be entreated: yields to reason.
- Mercifulness: not dead set on being right to the detriment of those deserving of mercy.
- Impartiality: not taking sides regardless of who is asking for the wisdom.
- A lack of hypocrisy: not two-faced or feigning.
- A commitment to doing the right thing the right way.

Common Sense and Specialized Wisdom

Common Sense: knowledge common to everyone without special training (however the authors acknowledge that not everyone has "common sense").

Specialized Wisdom: Moses required men skilled with gold, silver, brass, iron, and wood to build the tabernacle. See Isa. 22:13-16.

Skilled professionals: doctors, medical professionals, auto mechanics, librarians, lawyers etc.

Faith Building Practice and Review

1. How many steps are in the biblical process?

2. Commit them to memory.

3. Explain, in your own words, why it is so important to properly identify a problem.

4. Briefly explain the differences between earthly wisdom and wisdom from above.

5. What does it mean to *acknowledge the Lord in all thy ways?*

6. Practice the process, beginning with smaller decisions, then gradually working up to tougher issues. That way you won't become easily frustrated

7. Explain the difference between common sense and specialized wisdom.

8. Why is it so important to ask correct or vital questions?

Notes

Notes

Lesson 4

Hearing God's Voice

It's often been said, "God moves in mysterious ways." However, I believe that's incorrect. As biblical history shows, God always lets his people know what he's going to do long *before* He actually does it.

Principle: Amos 3:7 "Surely the Lord God will do nothing, but he revealeth his secret unto his servants the prophets."

Just read the prophecies concerning the Messiah's birth, death, burial and resurrection. That's proof positive that God always lets us know aforetime of upcoming events and consequences.

Diverse People to Whom God Spoke (Not an exhaustive list)

- Gen. 2:16-3:24: Adam walked and conversed with God before the fall
- Gen. 4:6-15: God's dialogue with Cain (shows God reaching out to fallen man)
- Gen. 5:22: Enoch walked with God (shows relationship)
- Gen. 6-9: God's relationship and dialogue with Noah

- Gen. 12-22: God's relationship and dialogue with Abraham and his posterity
- Num. 22:22-35: God speaks to Balaam's ass/donkey then to Balaam
- 1Kings 19:4-18 the Lord speaks to Elijah, the prophet, in a *still small voice*
- Acts 9:1-9 Saul's encounter with Jesus on the road to Damascus
- 2 Peter1:20-21 God spoke "as they were *moved* by the Holy Ghost"
- Acts10:9-20 the Spirit speaks to Peter concerning the vision Peter had
- Acts 2:16-18 prophesies by sons and daughters, visions, dreams
- John10:3-5 Jesus said, that His sheep know his voice and follow him and not a stranger.

He Lives

How can we sing the song: "He lives, He lives, Christ Jesus lives today! He walks with me and talks with me along life's narrow way"—if we don't hear His voice? You can say or sing the words without hearing or realizing (or caring) what they mean!

John10:1-5 clearly states that "His sheep hear His voice." Not His pastors only, or just certain individuals. But rather *all* the sheep of His pasture will know and follow His voice, meaning that God will make certain that you know his voice. But you must ask, and then listen.

The Guidelines

1. The voice you hear must not violate or run amiss of sound theology and methodology of interpretation. While the specifics are not usually found "written in the word," the principles are, and must always be, fully supported by the written word by precept and example.

2. The message from the voice must, and always will, come to pass exactly as spoken.
3. The child of God must develop and maintain a deep relationship with the Lord through an ongoing daily basis of worship, praise, and reading and study of the Word. Maintaining the relationship is not an option, nor is it to be done haphazardly. If God does not hear from you, how and why should you hear from Him?
4. God's voice will never violate or transgress His written Word.
5. The voice you hear will never violate God's character.

Ask for Wisdom

Principle: James 1:5-7 "If any of you lack wisdom, let him ask of God, that giveth to all men liberally, and upbraideth not; and it shall be given him. But let him ask in faith, nothing wavering. For he that wavereth is like a wave of the sea driven with the wind and tossed. For let not that man think that he shall receive any thing of the Lord."

Diverse Methods and Ways of Hearing God's Voice

Author's note: No one hears God the same way as any one else, nor does His voice sound the same, but there are methods and ways to hear His voice.

- Ma• ny have heard from God without knowing or acknowledging the fact. 1Sam. 3:1-10
- Many simply don't believe God speaks to his people.
- Others believe God only speaks through
- Special people such as pastors or evangelists.
- Few have been taught how to hear God's voice, and even fewer have heard a teaching about hearing God's voice, even in seminaries.

Here is a list of ways and methods we'll study. Many may work in conjunction with each other at the same time.

> The written Word: Psalm 119:105, 130
> The spoken Word: 1Cor. 14:1-40
> Nature/creation: Psalm19:1-4; Rom. 1:20
> Conviction and guidance: John 16:7*13
> Inner witness/still small voice: 1Kings 19: 9-13; Rom. 8:14-16, 26
> Supernatural revelation and prophesy: Gne. 40 and 41; Joseph's dreams: Joel 2:28; 1Cor.14:3
> Wisdom: Prov. 1:2-9; James 1:5-8; 3:17-18
> Godly counsel: Prov.11:14; 15:22; James 3:17-18
> Disbelievers: Num. 22:21-33
> Inner Peace: John 14:27; Rom. 8:6
> Two or three witnesses: Deut. 17:6; Matt. 18:16; 2 Cor. 2:13

Remember, none of these methods will ever violate even one of the guidelines previously listed.

Principle: 2 Peter1:20-21 "Knowing this first that no prophecy of the scripture is of private interpretation For the prophecy came not in old time by the will of man: but holy men of God spake, as they were moved by the Holy Ghost." In other words, the Scriptures are not the figment of someone's imagination.

The Still Small Voice

Principle: 1Kings 19:11-13 "And he said, go on, and stand upon the mount before the Lord. And, behold the Lord passed by, and a great strong wind rent the mountains, and broke in pieces the rocks before the Lord, but the Lord was not in the wind: and after the wind an earthquake; but the Lord was not in the earthquake: and after the earthquake a fire; but the Lord was not in the fire: and after the fire a still small voice. And it was so, when Elijah heard it, he wrapped himself in his mantle and went out, and stood in the entrance of the cave. And, behold, there came a voice unto him and said . . ."

Each of us is bombarded daily with emotional firestorms which may block out the voice of God.

Author's Note: It is my personal belief, though not supported by scripture, that the wind, earthquake and fire in 1Kings.19:11-12 represent the powerful emotions a person experiences in life, especially during extreme trials!

The key is to "learn" the voice of God, even as Elijah did not act until *after* the wind, earthquake, and fire (emotional turmoil). It was when he heard the "still small voice" that he got up and continued. Before Elijah ran for his life, into the wilderness, he was able to hear God's voice. It was only after Jezebel's edict that his emotions became so overwhelming that he could no longer discern God's voice.

Principle: 1Cor.6:17 "But he that is joined unto the Lord is one spirit."

In the New Testament, God's children, those who have been born of the Spirit, (John 3:6b), are one spirit with the Lord and thus able to hear God's "still small voice" in their spirit. It is not a voice of emotional outbursts. Rather it is a voice that one can only hear when one is quiet in one's spirit. Therefore it is of utmost importance to get quiet in your spirit to hear God's voice.

Author's Note: It is impossible to commune with God through the flesh. It must be through the Spirit. John4:24, Rmm. 8:16, 1Cor. 6:17

Jesus told the woman at the well: John 4:24 "God is a Spirit: and they that worship him must worship him in spirit and in truth," not the flesh. Communing with God is a form of worship.

Inner Witness

Principle: Romans 8:16 "The Spirit itself bears witness with our spirit, that we are the children of God."

Principle: 2 Peter 1:20-21 "Knowing this first, that no prophecy of the scripture is of private interpretation. For the prophecy came not in old time by the will of man: but holy men of God spoke, as they were moved by the Holy Ghost."

Principle: 1Corinthians 6:17 "But he that is joined unto the Lord is one spirit." This passage demonstrates that there is a distinct "still small voice" which can also be called the witness of the Spirit (God) with our spirit (human).

Remember, you are joined unto the Lord by spirit. Your human spirit is joined or espoused to the Holy Spirit through baptism of the Spirit. Therefore, the inner voice you hear is that of the Spirit communing or speaking to your human spirit.

That is why it is so important to "be still and know that I am God" (Psalm 46:10).

My Sheep Know My Voice

Principle: John 10:3-5 Jesus said. "My sheep know my voice."

Are you a part of God's flock? Are you one of the sheep of his pasture? Do you not know your Shepherd's voice? The only way to learn God's voice is to spend time alone with Him in prayer, study, worship, and praise. In fact, there are no absolute methods dictated in scripture, only guidelines. The most important requirement to learn God's voice is that it must be in spirit and truth. A liar simply cannot worship or commune with God, for it is contrary to God's nature and character to lie.

Principle: John 4:21-23 "in spirit and truth" Remember his principle: "sheep know his voice and will not follow another voice" (John10:4-5).

We are to worship "in spirit and truth."

Reason and Rationalization

Principle: Proverbs 3:5-6 "Trust in the Lord with all thine heart; and lean not unto thine own understanding. In all thy ways acknowledge Him, and He shall direct thy paths."

As humans, we are naturally wired for, or given to, reason, attempting to rationalize almost everything. However, when God speaks to you, He will leave no doubt in your mind and spirit that it was, in fact, Him. Abraham went to the mountain, upon hearing God's instruction, to offer the sacrifice of Isaac, for he knew it was the voice of his God. He did not try to rationalize or reason what God said.

Sheep of His Pasture

Principle: John 10:3-5 "To him the porter opens; and the sheep hear his voice: and he calls his own sheep by name, and leads them out. And when he putteth forth his own sheep, he goes before them, and the sheep follow him: for they know his voice. And a stranger they will not follow, but will flee from him: for they know not the voice of strangers."

Clearly this passage speaks of an individual's intimate relationship with God, so intimate that His voice is known. They were in His presence continually enjoying His fellowship, protection, and provision, so much so that they knew His voice! He actually spoke to each and every one individually, not through another person! That's powerful!

Two or Three Witnesses

Principle: Deuteronomy 19:16-20; Matthew 18:16 ". . . At the mouth of two or three witnesses shall a matter be established."

Note that these and other similar passages are primarily speaking of bringing witness for the purpose of establishing guilt or innocence in a court of law. Even so, they must be credible witnesses and not bring false testimony.

If one or more persons bring a similar, unsolicited message from the Lord, it ought to be a confirmation in your spirit of what God has already told you. If not it may be a false testimony.

Events and Life's Circumstances

I have come to know God's voice through various circumstances. For example, after an accident in which my car was rear-ended by a semi, the family and I went shopping for another vehicle. I must say that of all the cars and trucks I've purchased in over forty years of driving, I've never encountered so many literal "lemons"! One car died on the highway while test driving. One had been rear-ended so hard it literally shoved the front end into something, but the repairs were noticeable only to the trained eye. Still another one had been T-boned, and the repairs were shabby, to say the least. Still another one had evidence of being stolen and vandalized. Yet none of problems found in these "fine" automobiles had been reported. Soon, I began to pay attention and perceived that God was telling me not to car shop. That was correct, for very shortly the doctors forbade me from driving either my personal car or the buses I drove at work, or even riding a bicycle for at least three months. What would have happened if I'd disobeyed or ignored God's voice? We'd be stuck with another car payment, plus insurance coupled together with no paycheck for several months. Learn to be still and listen for God's voice. Then obey!

What Does God Say to Us?

I believe, as stated earlier, that the message we receive from God will never violate His written Word. The messages are based on His Word.

Principle: James 1:5 "If any of you lacks wisdom, let him ask of God that gives to all men liberally, and upbraids not: and it shall be given him."

1) "Any of you" refers to any child of God, not just a member of the clergy. I'm convinced that a good number of the clergy have never heard God's voice, nor do they believe God speaks to His people today. What makes me so sure is that the actions of the person giving the wisdom prove to be those of the flesh and not the Spirit. James3:15-16 set forth the criteria for discerning between the wisdom of the flesh and the wisdom from above.

2) Asking is a definite form of communication, and commands a response. This is not to say we can *demand* that God do or say anything. Rather it is a request by which God has bound himself, by his written Word, to answer.

3) "God gives to all men liberally" is a direct, definitive method of communication, the promise of answered prayer.

Principle: Psalm 73:24 "Thou shall guide me with thy counsel, and afterward receive me to glory."

As noted, our guidance comes through the counsel of the Lord, which never violates the written Word. However, some mistakenly believe it means that God only quotes Scripture, when in fact He does give counsel by speaking to your spirit. He will give guidance and direction in perfect harmony with his written Word. For example, He may counsel you to hold your peace when you really want to lash out at someone. Or He may counsel you to take another route home or to the store, etc. You most likely will not understand why. Frequently you may never know. But you must do it anyway! Often reasons are not given by God. He just says "No." Eventually you'll find out why not!

4) He may counsel you to avoid getting involved with certain individuals for various reasons. He wants you know the pitfalls of such relationships. Hopefully you will wait for Him to speak.

Wisdom—Its Benefits

Godly Counsel

- ➤ Know wisdom and instruction, perceive understanding (Povr.1:2)
- ➤ Receive instruction of wisdom, justice, judgment, equity (Prov.1:3)
- ➤ Give subtlety to the simple minded and knowledge and discretion to young men (Prov.1:4)
- ➤ Attain wise/Godly counsel (Prov.1:5b)
- ➤ Understand proverbs and interpretations (Prov.1:6a)
- ➤ Be preserved (Prov.2:11)
- ➤ Be delivered from evil men and women (Prov.2:12, 16)
- ➤ Extend life and gain peace, (Prov.3:2)
- ➤ Gain favor with God and man (Prov. 3:4)
- ➤ Obtain health (Prov.3:8)
- ➤ Achieve wealth (Prov. 3:10)
- ➤ Attain happiness (Prov. 3:13)

Wisdom—Where it's Found

- ➤ In the streets (Prov. 1:20). Literally where we live—basically anywhere and everywhere you look and everywhere you are presently.
- ➤ Chief places, gates of the city (Prov.1:21). Today these would be our halls of justice.
- ➤ Virtually anywhere in the Bible.
- ➤ Godly counsel (Povr. 11:14; 15:22; 20:18; Ex. 18:19; 1Kings 12:7; Dan. 4:27; Psalm 16:7; 73:24; Isa. 11:2; 28:29; Je. 32:19; Re. 3:18)
- ➤ God gives wisdom liberally, to all who ask (James1:5).

The Two Wisdoms

James 3:13-16 outlines the products of earthly, sensual, devilish wisdom

➤ Bitter envy
➤ Strife
➤ Confusion
➤ Evil work

James 3:17-18 outlines products of wisdom from above/Godly wisdom

➤ Purity
➤ Peaceableness
➤ Gentleness
➤ Ability to be entreated
➤ Mercifulness
➤ Impartiality
➤ Absence of hypocrisy
➤ Righteousness

Note: verses 17-18 are partly descriptive of God's character; the opposite of earthly wisdom.

According to James 3:13-18, if you first seek a wise person, described in vs. 13, then that wisdom is from above! In other words, from God! For God speaks through wise people whose lives mirror James 3:13.

The Voice of Creation

Principle: Psalm 19:1-4a "The heavens declare the glory of God; and the firmament shows his handiwork. Day unto day utters speech and night unto night shows knowledge. There is no speech nor language, where their voice is not heard. Their line is gone out through all the earth and their words to the end of the world."

Have you ever gazed into the heavens on a warm summer day or night, and pondered the wonders of creation? I used to lie on my back, in a field, and be awestruck at the cloud formations, sun, and of the grass and trees—that was God's creation speaking volumes to me.

Principle: Rom.1:19-20 "Because that which may be known of God is manifest known in them; for God has shown it unto them. For the invisible things of him from the creation of the world are clearly seen, being understood by the things that are made, even his eternal power and Godhead, so that they are without excuse."

To me, this is on a parallel with Psalm19:1-4a. Creation is a vivid demonstration of God's power!

Many people simply cannot begin to believe in a divine creator, let alone a giver and sustainer of life. (However, the above passages clearly declare the glory and power of God to all men in the world, thus leaving all without excuse.)The voice of creation declares the following:

➤ God's glory
➤ God's handiwork (creation not evolution)
➤ God's power/great authority (omnipotence)
➤ God's presence (omnipresence)
➤ God's righteousness
➤ God's wrath

Caution must be exercised not to confuse nature and creation as being the Lord God. In other words, many begin to worship the creation rather than the Creator!

Many times, God will whisper something in your spirit concerning changes that need to be made in your personal life. You need these quiet, personal communications or counsels from Him to grow in the inner person.

He has told me to change a certain type of behavior and given me solid reasons to change, warning of the negative consequences if I don't change.

He has whispered/counseled me to avoid certain individuals or circumstances citing various pitfalls or disobediences. He has even uttered directives for me to speak to others concerning something that concerns them.

For example, an elderly lady in her mid-nineties was in a nursing home with a terrible staph infection in her leg. She had been in and out of the hospital and rehab care for more than six months. Her daughter, from New Mexico, wanted to take her mother to the doctor and meet him. However, she met with resistance and excuses time after time. The Lord told me to tell the daughter to ask the Lord to walk before her the next day in order for her to meet and visit the doctor. So she did. When she arrived at the doctor's office, the nurse bluntly told her the doctor was booked for a month and that it was his day off. Then the nurse looked up and saw the doctor hanging up his coat, so the daughter went over, introduced herself and the doctor saw her mother immediately.

Ask, Seek, and Knock

> Matthew 7:7 "Ask and it shall be given you; seek and ye shall find; knock, and it shall be opened unto you."

Perhaps the place where we fail the most is in failing to ask, to seek, to knock. By doing these things, God will teach us to hear His voice.

God's Voice or Satan's Voice?

Principle: John 10:3-4 " . . . and the sheep hear his voice: and he calls his own sheep by name, and leads them out. And when he puts forth his own sheep, he goes before them, and the sheep follow him: for they know his voice."

God has ways to insure we recognize His voice; however, we can and do often miss hearing it if we do not know how to listen, or just plain don't listen. But He never leaves it to chance.

The following is a list of the differences between God's voice and Satan's voice. By studying the list, we can begin to recognize God's voice and learn to do His will.

Fruit of God's Voice:

John10:3-16
> - Leads
> - Saves, feeds
> - Gives life
> - Gathers/protects/nurtures
> - Sacrifices/gives life for sheep's good

James3:17-18
> - Is pure
> - Is peaceable
> - Is gentle
> - Is easy to be entreated
> - Is full of mercy
> - Is without partiality
> - Is without hypocrisy
> - Is righteous

Author's Note: Notice how many voices there are for Satan, versus the number for God

Fruit of Satan's Voice:

1 John 10:3-16
> - Robs
> - Steals
> - Kills
> - Destroys
> - Scatters

James 3:13-16

> - Is earthly
> - Is sensual
> - Is devilish
> - Is bitterly envious

- ➢ Fosters strife
- ➢ Promotes evil works
- ➢ Incites confusion

2 Peter 2:9-22
- ➢ Walks after flesh/lust or uncleanness
- ➢ Despises governments
- ➢ Is presumptuous
- ➢ Is self-willed
- ➢ Speaks evil of dignitaries
- ➢ Lacks understanding
- ➢ Is pleasured to riot in daytime
- ➢ Is self-deceived
- ➢ Is adulterous
- ➢ Cannot cease from sin
- ➢ Beguiles/tricks unstable souls
- ➢ Engages in covetous practices
- ➢ Loves the wages of unrighteousness

God *always* leads by peace! Peace of mind, soul, and body, thus leaving you void of anxiety. He never leads by coercion, intimidation, guilt, force, intellect, anger, fear, manipulation, or emotions. He *only* leads by peace.

Faith-Building Practice and Review

1. Do you know the voice of God?

2. Why is it so important to learn to hear His voice?

3. List several other passages that have to do with hearing God's voice.

4. Study each passage carefully and prayerfully.

5. Do you know how to get quiet before God?

6. Practice getting quiet before Him three days this week.

7. Ask Him to make His voice known unto you.

8. Learn to get quiet in your spirit before Him. That means to ask Him to bring peace to your troubled soul and spirit, to not allow distractions and emotional turmoil to block His voice.

9. Compare the "voice" you hear with the lists that describe the differences between God's voice, your flesh, and Satan' voices.

10. Which voice do they most emulate? Why?

11. Does the "voice" you hear, agree with the written Word or violate it? Explain.

12. What does this mean: "it is impossible to commune with God in the flesh; it must be through the spirit"?

Notes

Lesson 5

Rash and Hasty Decisions

Definitions:

Hasty: "unduly quick; moving or acting with haste; brief, superficial."

Rash: "tending to act too hastily or without due consideration.".[3]

Emotional roller-coasters: are just that; emotional ups and downs which come in the forms of grief, joy, ecstasy, happiness, triumph, jubilation, humiliation, embarrassment, insult, pain, suffering, anger, disgust, discouragement, fatigue, etcetera, all vacillating back and forth.

Part of the problem we face today is that we are always in a hurry to do something or to get somewhere. Worse, we are literally overloaded in our schedules, and don't take the time to *stop* and *listen* for that "still small voice of God."

Principle: Ecclesiastes 5:1-7 "be not rash with thy mouth, and let not thine heart be hasty to utter anything before God." Don't get in too big a hurry!

---

[3] Random House Dictionary of the English Language, (1965), 605, 1095

Usually this happens when we are rushed to make a quick decision. Quite often it will happen when we are exhausted, irritated, confused, fearful, panicky, or otherwise emotionally distraught. When we are stressed out or tired, our minds become clouded and unstable, unable to think clearly. Our ability for reasoning is greatly impaired, not to mention that it is almost impossible to hear from God in this state. This is a dangerous time to make decisions. *Slow down!*

Remember, God is never in a hurry. He is always right on time! Chances are that if you are in a hurry, it is not God's time! Learn to get on God's time. Reset your spiritual watch!

Principle: Remember Ecclesiastes 3:1-11: "To everything there is a season and a time to every purpose under heaven." You can do the right thing at the wrong time and it can spell disaster

Author's note: One of my personal principles is never to make a decision without taking time to properly investigate. I try not to let anyone pressure me into a premature or emotional decision.

Emotions are a fact of life. However we should never make decisions based on emotion. Instead, we must allow the emotions to *wash over us*, however long that may take, and refrain from making decisions, especially major decisions, until we have had time to go through the decision-making process.

Elijah

Read 1 K.ings19:1-13. The passage tells us when Elijah, the prophet, came down from Mount Carmel, he became greatly distressed and depressed, to the point of ending his life because Jezebel had put a contract on his head for the slaying of 450 prophets of Baal. He ran into the wilderness and fasted for forty days and forty nights and cleared his head. Afterward, he saw a strong wind, fire, and earthquake, but God's voice was not in them. After the wind, fire, and earthquake, he heard a "still small voice" which was the voice of God.

The bottom line is that you have to stop and take inventory of yourself and listen to what your body is telling you! It may very well be *screaming* at you to *stop, slow down and listen* for God's "still small voice." To do that, you have to get quiet in your flesh and spirit to hear God's voice.

What happens when you make a bad decision? Let's face it, sometimes it does happen. Instead of going down with the ship, stop and get centered in the Lord once again, then proceed to correct the bad decision. Remember, your family is dependent on you (and your spouse) to make good, Godly decisions, as well as to come to a Godly solution to a poorly made decision.

All decisions should be motivated by love: love of God's Word, love of your fellow man, and last, but perhaps most important, the love of yourself.

Principle: Ecclesiastes 5:1-4 "Keep thy foot when thou goest to the house of God, and be more ready to hear, than to give the sacrifice of fools: for they consider not that they do evil. Be not rash with thy mouth, and let not thine heart be hasty to utter anything before God: for God is in heaven and thou upon the earth: therefore let thy words be few. For a dream cometh through the multitude of business; and a fool's voice is known by multitude of words. When thou vowest a vow unto God, defer not to pay it; for he hath no pleasure fools: pay that which thou hast vowed." This is a clear admonition for us to think seriously before we make a vow or promise.

Jephthah (An example of hasty a decision)

> Judges 11:30-31 "There was a man named Jephthah who vowed a vow unto God, that whatever was to come through the door he would offer up to God as a burnt offering."

Jephthah was a godly man who gave no forethought to his hasty decision to offer a burnt offering to the Lord. Afterward, when he saw his daughter come through the door, he was very sorrowful; nevertheless he fulfilled his vow unto God.

Principle: Ecclesiastes 5:1-4 states that we are not to "be hasty with our vows with God . . . for God has no pleasure in fools."

Ignorance and Impulse: Ignorance is the absence of knowledge, while impulse is making a sudden decision based on a wish or an urge. Often they are found together like Siamese twins. For example; you may purchase a car simply because you like the color, but you fail to check out its performance records, only to find out later it is a gas hog, costing you tons of money to feed. Or it may have a history of mechanical problems.

Principle: In Genesis 16:1-6, Abrahm's wife, Sarai, made a rash decision to allow Abrahm to father a child with Hagar, her servant. Afterward Sarai became very jealous, and hated Hager and her child, and eventually banished them out of her house and sight. Abrahm should not have listened to her, and that was his mistake.

In my opinion, both Abrahm and Sarai acted hastily. On the one hand, they attempted to fulfill God's promise of a son, while not fully thinking through the act they both entered into.

Faith Building Practice and Review

1. What is the difference between ignorance-based and impulsive decision-making?

2. List three decisions you made out of ignorance.

3. Now list their outcomes, positive or negative.

4. List three decisions you made on impulse.

5. Now list their outcomes, positive or negative.

6. Do you see them working together against you or for you? Explain.

7. Reread all the principles, including my personal ones, and write them down.

8. When was the last time you made a decision based on your emotions?

9. Do you recall those emotions? If so, write them down.

10. Do you recall how your body behaved? For example, did it exhibit nervousness, doubt, anger, an upset stomach, clenched fists, nail-biting, etc.?

11. Now that you have identified some of your body's language or feelings while making decisions, think of ways to overcome the emotion and practice every time you get in a position to make a decision. For instance, you might try leaving the scene for a while until you calm yourself and return later, (it took Elijah forty days and forty nights of fasting and praying to calm himself), or you might try taking several deep breaths, and holding them for five or ten seconds. Experiment until you find what works for you.

12. Briefly explain how those emotional decisions turned out.

13. Can you list the times in the last month you acted out of haste?

14. Three months?

15. Six months?

16. One year?

17. What do these say about your skills as a decision-maker?

18. You would like to change, wouldn't you?

Notes

Lesson 6

Do I Want It or Need It?

Principle: Proverbs 22:4 "The rich ruleth over the poor, and the borrower is servant to the lender." You are contractually obligated to repay a lender with interest, meaning that you are subject to the obligations of the contract.

Principle: Luke 12:15 "And he said unto them, Take heed, and beware of covetousness: for a man's life consisteth not in the abundance of the things, which he possesseth."

Needs or wants are areas that often cause great turmoil in family relationships, and require a great deal of insight into the emotional states underlying the perceived need or want. The solution requires self discipline until a Godly decision can be made. Countless times a day we are made subject to seducement, to part with our hard earned money. The lure of the latest state-of-the-art gizmo is powerful. After all, just how many can openers do you *need?* Not to mention how many can you use?

When my parents commenced to glory they were still using the same cast aluminum pots and pans with wooden handles they received as wedding gifts over sixty-five years before. And you know what? They still worked just fine! I don't think they ever owned an electric can opener. They still used the hand operated one. You know, the one you hold in one hand while twisting the butterfly handle with the other, as the blade grinds its way in a circle around the lid of the can! Their back-up can opener had a wire corkscrew, for wine bottles, tucked neatly inside the handle.

The culture we live in quite literally thrives on debt! Debt is what makes the world go around, and without it there would be little progress made in the world.

Think of it. Before the great depression, from 1929 through the early 1940s, I'm told that nearly 80 percent of American families owned their homes outright. Afterward, came the great push for credit and indebtedness. As a result, today only approximately 20 percent of Americans own their houses outright! Shocking isn't it?

Everything is centered on the idea that someone can take the hard-earned money out of your pocket and place it into his own. Because no one person has the talent, time or ability to manufacture every necessity in their life, greed and debt have become the foundation of the medium of exchange. There is nothing inherently wrong with accumulating material possessions. However, accumulating possessions in excess may cause a person to shift his worship from the Living God to the accumulation of "things."

The issue before us in this chapter is to decipher the difference between a *want* and a *need*.

Advertisements are most often centered or focused on celebrity appeal, sex appeal, or alcohol. Why? Simply because the advertisement industry, long ago, figured out that these three things appeal to us and arouse desires or perceived needs within each of us.

For example:

- Celebrity appeal: caters to our basic need to "be someone," or to identity with the famous. So to make a purchase of whatever, solely because celebrity so-and-so is touting it, somehow makes the product or service credible, reliable, and worthy of our ownership.
- Sex appeal: a half-naked, youthful woman, with a voluptuous body standing next to the fender of an

automobile, makes a man want to purchase that car. Youthful, appealing persons of either sex, who demonstrate kitchen countertops, garbage disposers, and storm doors, make us want to open our wallets and purchase those products.

- Alcohol: what is there about alcohol that makes people want to open their wallets?

Have you noticed that none of the above-mentioned gimmicks really has anything to do with the product or service?

The retail industry spends millions of dollars each year on research to discover a better way to "pick your pocket" and still have you enjoy it! They know how to scratch you right where you itch! They know your likes, dislikes, weaknesses, strengths, even your buying cycles.

They know when you bought that new Jet Ski, and when you bought the last one three years ago. They are pros, projecting your buying cycle for every three years, so they can "hit" you up for another one at regular intervals, with all the latest technology and gadgetry! Guess what? You're hooked! Never mind that you can't afford the thing! In fact you probably still owe on the last one! So how do you beat the system?

How do you distinguish between a need and a want?
It depends on the situation.

When I had my own business as a farrier, I needed a pickup truck to carry the weight of all my tools and equipment. What I did not need was a four-wheel drive, with captain's seats and a host of other amenities. At first, I bought used vehicles. Later on I needed better, more reliable and lasting transportation. My first new pickup was a three-quarter ton, with a big V8 engine, A/C and four-speed manual transmission, extended cab (great for taking my young kids along), and AM/FM stereo.

From then on, I thought every truck ought to have exactly the same features—that is, until I priced the new models seven years later and found I not only did not need the extended cab, big V8 engine, AM/FM stereo and A/C, but also that it suited my needs just fine to settle for less: a six cylinder, AM/FM radio, no A/C, and no dome light. Oh, to be sure it would have been nice to have all those extras, but not at the financial expense! You see, in that seven year period, the price for the truck with the lesser amenities was the same price as the one seven years earlier with all the trimmings!

Still later, when I retired from my business, I wanted another truck, (I loved driving and owning them!), but I could not justify the need for one. So, after my family "sat" on me a few times and reminded me of my many lectures to our sons about needs verses wants, I finally gave in to a small sized 1997 Geo Prizm, which, by the way, served me well for several years. That is, until the semi totaled it in 2006! I told the boys, now grown men, to decide what kind of vehicle they needed to accomplish whatever they wanted it to do. Why buy a semi when a small sized Toyota pickup would be all they needed and then some? If they needed a truck, it needed to pay for itself. Still I have the hankering to drive a pickup from time to time, but alas, I must take my own medicine, lest I be a hypocrite! For my current needs, it's cheaper and makes more sense to rent or borrow one, rather than buy something I can't afford or will only use once a year.

Most of us have our garages so full of stuff that the cars sit in the driveway or street! Some even rent storage units to store their ever-rotting "treasures." Ouch! That hurt!

Principle: Matthew 6:19-21 "Lay not up for yourselves treasures upon earth, where moth and rust doth corrupt, and where thieves break through and steal: but lay up for yourselves treasures in heaven, where neither moth nor rust doth corrupt and where thieves do not break through nor steal; for where your treasure is there your heart will be also."

This is not an edict against earthly goods or treasure. Rather, I see it as a statement for moderation and having your heart in the right place. Certainly a lot of Old Testament people such as Abraham, Job, and Kings David and Solomon acquired an abundance of material wealth, but they did not let it distract them from worshipping and serving God.

I spent seven years in the financial services industry, and I saw people of all ages, genders, cultures and ethnic backgrounds making terrible financial decisions, mostly based on wants instead of needs. Even worse, it was very difficult to sit down with them and show them how to get out of debt! Most were sacrificing their retirement years by not investing, but spending their money on wants! They just didn't "get it!"

Author's Note: We had a true saying in the office: "You can't spend your way to prosperity!"

Principle: Romans 13:8 "Owe no man anything, but to love one another: for he that loveth another hath fulfilled the law."

The thrust here is to love your fellow man and not become indebted to material things. In other words, having things is not bad in and of itself, but borrowing to accumulate those things puts you in the position of a slave, and the lender can take you to court for failure to make timely and proper payments.

People are driving huge gas guzzling SUVs and monster vehicles and can't even afford to put gas in the tank. Why? I read somewhere that some even torch the vehicles when they can't make the payments or buy gas, so they can collect the insurance money!

People buy over-priced houses with insufficient incomes to support themselves or their mansion. Why? It is because they failed to distinguish between *needs* and *wants*. Then they blame society, or worse yet, they blame God, but they rarely blame themselves!

Needs or *wants* can literally make or break a marriage (or a business) financially, and eventually the relationship itself. Both partners need to openly discuss and determine their *needs* and *wants*. If you *want* a dozen children, but can only afford one or two, then you *need* to adjust your priorities, or risk living in poverty, each working a multitude of jobs, hiring sitters and/or daycare centers.

Diane and I decided it was more economical and practical for her to stay at home with our young son until school age, and live on one income, than to have her work and pay for a sitter or day care.

Author's Note: Sometimes our fondest dreams can become our worst nightmares if not wisely and prudently acquired.

Instead of buying a brand new, ten bedroom, six bathroom mansion while flipping hamburgers at the Golden Arches Restaurant for minimum wage when you're starting out, why not rent a small apartment for a few years until you've managed to save enough for a nice down payment and have moved up the food chain to perhaps a franchise owner. Then you can start with a small one or two bedroom, one bathroom bungalow for a few years, then trade up until you can hopefully afford that ten-bedroom, six-bathroom mansion of your dreams.

Faith-Building Practice and Review

For these questions, please refer to the "Column Method" in lesson 2 and use the "Notes" section at the end of this lesson and/or a separate sheet of paper.

1. As an individual, sit down and make a list of needs you think you cannot function without, or needs without which your health would be put at risk. For instance, dental care, including regular cleaning, etc., or perhaps regular maintenance on your cars. Then list the positive and negative effects, both of having and not having them.

2. Now, make a list of things you really don't *need*, but *want,* almost as badly as if they were a necessity. Then list the pros and cons. Now, with your spouse, as a couple, compare your lists, share your concerns and make decisions over which needs to keep and which to eliminate. Don't fight! Ask God!

When high definition television became the norm, Diane and I discussed the pros and cons of purchasing a new television, at a considerably higher cost, as opposed to a ten-dollar converter box to convert the old television set from analog to high definition. We settled on the converter box, concluding that we could save money, as we did not use all the channels from our television provider. We settled for fewer channels, with the quality of more expensive high definition televisions.

3. As a single person, it is advisable for you to consult with a few mature, trusted friends, or relatives, to assist you.

4. As a couple, make an agreement to discuss whether or not that new "thing-a-ma-jig" is a necessity or a want.

5. When in doubt, pass by the item or think about it. Sometimes holding onto the item and conversing with yourself (self-talk) will give you time to decide rationally. Ask yourself, "Do I have something similar to it? Would this money be put to better use elsewhere?"

Each person needs a discretionary income, in equivalent amounts for a couple, even if the spouse doesn't work. This will help to cut down on feelings of anger or resentment. But when an individual decides to spend his discretionary income, he needs to be able to discern between a need and a want. For example, I have a great difficulty passing up a bargain on tools! Do I need them or want them? It's my discretionary money! This cuts down on feelings of anger or resentment.

Notes

Do I Want It or Need It?

Notes

Lesson 7

Finances and Retirement

Financial decisions are among the top problem areas for people of all ages. Either they ignore basic financial principles or they are simply ignorant of them.

Principle: Hosea 4:6a "My people are destroyed for lack of knowledge: because thou hast rejected knowledge, I will also reject thee."

Either a lack of knowledge or the rejection of knowledge can be devastating at any age. The irony of it is you may earnestly and sincerely claim ignorance, but the fact is that "ignorance is no excuse." That means your ignorance or rebellion will not and cannot reverse or withhold the consequences of financial ineptness. It is up to you and me to research and discover the facts and principles for our own good.

Ignorance Is No Excuse

Principle: Leviticus4:2 "Speak unto the children of Israel, saying, If a soul shall sin through *ignorance* against any of the commandments of the Lord concerning things which ought not to be done, and shall do against any of them: if the priest that is anointed do sin according to the sin of the people; let him bring for his sin, which he hath sinned, a young bullock without blemish unto the Lord for a sin offering."

Author's Note: ignorance is no excuse. For example: there are countless laws on the books, in our cities, states and country, that we, individually, may not be aware of. We, nevertheless, are still accountable for obeying these laws. (Although how we find out about some of them may not be pleasant!)

Author's note: I find it interesting that "ignore" and "ignorant" are from the same root word, "ignore." While "ignorant" denotes a lack of knowledge, "ignore" demonstrates a rebellion, in refusal to see, or rejects acquired knowledge.

Stewardship with Finances

Principle: Luke 12:42-48 "And the Lord said, Who then is that faithful and wise steward, whom his lord shall make ruler over his household, to give them their portion of meat in due season? Blessed is that servant, whom his lord when he cometh shall find so doing. Of a truth I say unto you, that he will make him ruler over all that he hath. But and if that servant say in his heart, My lord delayeth his coming; and shall begin to beat the menservants and maidens, and to eat and drink, and to be drunken; the lord of that servant will come in a day when he looketh not for him, and at an hour when he is not aware, and will cut him in sunder, and will appoint him his portion with the unbelievers. And that servant, which knew his lord's will, and prepared not himself, neither did according to his will, shall be beaten with many stripes. But he who knew not, and did commit things worthy of stripes, shall be beaten with few stripes. For unto whomsoever much is given, of him shall much be required: and to whom men have committed much, of him will they ask the more."

The faithful and prudent person will take every precaution to ensure financial stability. Nothing we have truly belongs to us— it is on loan to us by our heavenly Father. If you don't believe it, just observe a few funerals, and see how much the deceased takes with him and how much is left behind for others to use.

Principle: Luke 16:1-3, 8, 10 "And he said also unto his disciples, There was a rich man, which had a steward; and the same was accused unto him that he had wasted his goods And he called him, and said, How is it that I hear this of thee? Give an account of thy stewardship; for thou mayest be no longer steward Then the steward said within himself, What shall I do? For my lord taketh away from me the stewardship: I cannot dig; to beg I am ashamed. And the lord commended the unjust steward, because he had done wisely: for the children of this world are in their generation wiser than the children of light. He that is faithful in that which is least is faithful also in much: and he that is unjust in the least is unjust also in much."

Nothing belongs to any of us! It all belongs to God, the Creator, who places it in our hands to manage. Later, will we all have to give an account of our management skills? Read Luke16;1-13.

If we were better managers of God's property, then would we not be given more to manage? Read Matthew25:14-30.

Principle: Luke 16:10 "He that is faithful in that which is least is faithful also in much: and he that is unjust in the least is unjust also in much."

If you cannot handle the small amount given you, how can you expect to handle even more? Statistics show that the majority of lottery winners are broke within a very short period of time. Also, those who do many things well will be given more to do, and given the Lord's strength and wisdom to do the tasks, as well.

Principle: Matthew 25:24 "Then he which had received the one talent came and said, Lord, I knew thee that thou art an hard man, reaping where thou hast not sown, and gathering where thou hast not strawed."

The faithful servants who invested their lord's money and doubled it received a greater dominion to rule over. Whereas the foolish servant who hid his master's money had everything taken away from him! Read Matthew25:14-30.

Stewardship with God's Word

Principle: 1Corinthians 4:1-2 "Let a man so account of us, as of the ministers of Christ, and stewards of the mysteries of God. Moreover it is required in stewards, that a man be found faithful."

Principle: 1 Peter 4:10 "As every man has received the gift, even so minister the same one to another, as good stewards of the manifold grace of God."

The above passages refer to God's children being held accountable to God for the care of His people, and correctly dividing the word of truth. They do not refer to monetary issues.

How are you caring for God's people? How are you at hearing, sharing, and living God's Word? Are you faithful, or unfaithful?

Red Flags

Here are some red flags I've noticed in my life and in the lives of others as well.

- Lone Ranger decisions: that is, making large and vital financial decisions without first consulting your spouse, if married. It is of utmost importance to the strength and vitality of the marriage to consult with each other. You can also be accountable to a close friend or relative.
- Compulsive spending patterns: titillating advertisements, mood swings, or hormones often bring these on. We have both discovered that it's best not to go grocery shopping on an empty stomach or without a list. We have a list by the kitchen door that we each add to as needed.
- Failure to ask questions or the right questions: We ought to ask, how much are the monthly payments? What is

the interest? Also ask, what is the total cost, including interest? And, when will it be paid off?

- Prideful and arrogant or spiteful decisions: Sometimes we make purchases out of anger toward another person, just to "show them." Sometimes it gives a sense of pride in ownership for that new thing-a-ma-jig. Sometimes we haven't a clue of what it's for or how to use it; but, it sure feels good to have it!

- Emotional decisions: those made out of anger, revenge, insecurity, or fear.

- Wants vs. needs: this is a big one, as often there is a fine line between the two. Emotions can be a huge factor and have the tendency to blur or muddy decisions. Accountability to someone else will help eliminate and clear up these issues. The media plays a vital role in this arena. Emotions appeal to our vulnerable side, and our natural sense of greed! Sex and celebrity also sell, as they appeal, once again, to our vulnerable side!

- Putting all your eggs in one basket: not having a back-up job or profession; not diversifying your investments; counting only on your little nest egg for retirement. Most farmers were brought up with a sense of frugality and financial savvy, and therefore tend to set aside for that proverbial "rainy day." My brother-in-law and eldest sister were farmers and proved this concept to be true. My brother-in-law inherited the family farm and ran it quite well for many years before retiring. In the process, the farm provided for his aging parents in their retirement.

"God is not a fire escape to be used only in case of fire. He is into fire prevention. He would rather teach us to avoid setting fires than put out a 4-alarm fire in your personal life."
Richard Godfrey

- Denial: "I don't have a problem" or "I've got it under control." Be honest. If you continue to rack up huge debt that you know you can't afford to pay, you have to know you have a problem. Denying the fact does nothing to resolve it.

- Spending too much for basic items with little regard for comparison shopping. Once again I gained this insight from the stint in financial services. Diane is very good at comparison shopping.
- Miracles: *always* asking and depending on God to provide a miracle for your incompetence and rebellion instead of improving your knowledge and skills.

Author's Note: Many times God will withhold a "miracle" in favor of teaching us to obey His principles.

- Lottery, jackpots, bingo games and get rich quick schemes: the odds of losing are greater than the odds of winning.
- Chasing interest rates: refinancing your mortgage every time the interest rate lowers. There are better ways to save.
- Spending more time planning for vacation than for retirement: then start planning retirement twenty to thirty years late, or just before retirement time. OUCH!!!
- Mortgage payment in retirement: A retired neighbor in his middle eighties told me, "You can't retire and have a house payment." I think that's sound advice.
- Spending more than you earn: This is often accomplished through misuse and abuse of credit, usually without regard to the total expense with interest and penalties compounded!
- Emotional and impulse spending is a huge financial blunder!

Remember the parable of the fool who built his house upon the sand.

Principle: Matthew 7:24-27 "Therefore whosoever heareth these sayings of mine, and doeth them, I will liken him unto a wise man, which built his house upon a rock: and the rain descended, and the floods came, and the winds blew, and beat upon that house; and it fell not: for it was founded upon a rock. And everyone that heareth these sayings of mine, and doeth them not, shall be likened unto a foolish man, which built his house upon the sand: and the rain descended, and the floods came, and the winds blew, and beat upon that house; and it fell: and great was the fall of it."

The parable is not only applicable in reference to the salvation of the soul but also to poor decision making in many areas of life, including finances, and relationships.

Principle: Matthew 6:45b "For he maketh his sun to rise on the evil and on the good, and sendeth rain on the just and on the unjust."

God is so righteous that He provides for disbelievers as well as believers. So, wealth is not an indicator of right standing with God.

What Are Your Financial Patterns?

Everyone has them. Ask yourself:

- Am I aware of the financial mistakes I make over and over?
- Why do I make them?
- What can I do to change damaging habits?
- Do I have a pattern of waiting for a financial miracle to save me?
- Do I have a pattern of chasing mortgage interest rates and refinancing?
- How and to whom can I make myself accountable?

Principle: Hosea 4:6a "my people are destroyed for lack of knowledge."

Are you going to be destroyed for lack of knowledge or for the rejection of knowledge? The answer is to educate yourself on financial matters.

> ➤ There are books in the library we can use to research this subject, including books for different age groups, such as teens and seniors, giving sound financial advice.

Tithes and Offerings

Principle: Leviticus 27:30-32 "And all the tithe of the land, whether of the seed of the land, or of the fruit of the tree, is the Lord's: it is holy unto the Lord. And if a man will at all redeem ought of his tithes, he shall add thereto the fifth part thereof. And concerning the tithe or the herd, or of the flock, even whatsoever passeth under the rod, the tenth shall be holy unto the Lord."

Many do not believe in paying tithes and offerings to God or the church, but they deceive themselves and miss out on many blessings.

The Tithe Belongs To God

Principle: Malachi 3:8-9 "Will a man rob God? Yet ye have robbed me. But ye say, Wherein have we robbed thee? In tithes and offerings. Ye are cursed with a curse: for ye have robbed me, even this whole nation."

Why is it that some Christians don't seem to believe that not paying tithes is, in fact, robbing God?

While as a guest on a radio talk show, discussing my book, a lady called in asking, "What do you do about tithes when you don't have any money?" Sadly, there are a lot of Christians in that situation. My answer was to ask her what bad financial decisions had she made to position herself with no money for tithes? (Unfortunately we ran out of air time before I could better explain.) However, I believe that God's Word is true today. He will provide as we are faithful to obey His Word in tithing. As for those who may be in the unfortunate position of being almost penniless, might I suggest the story of the widow's mites in Mark12:41-44, in which the widow, being poor, still put the least that she had into the treasury and Jesus counted it as a form of worship, commending her.

Principle: Numbers 15:24a "Then it shall be, if ought to be committed by ignorance without the knowledge of the congregation, that the entire congregation shall offer one young bullock for a burnt offering."

God made a stipulation with Israel for the sin of ignorance. So, we also must pay for ignorant decisions! Yes, even ignorance of tithes and offerings. Remember, Rom. 1:19-20 and Psalm 9:1-4 that God puts his laws in our hearts and conscience to obey in the absence of formal teaching.

Author's Note: Be careful how you make decisions, as they often have far-reaching consequences. Biblical principles are still in effect today! The principles have never been done away with.

Some Frugal Tips

- Thrift stores, also known to some as "boutiques," are a great way to save on everything from clothing to garden tools and patio furniture. Of course you have to be selective to find a deal for you, but hey, you can literally save a bundle on name brand and designer clothes and merchandise. When our children were small, Diane would shop the "boutiques" for name brand clothes, as we knew they would outgrow the clothes long before they wore them out. Likewise, some of our own wardrobes are often from "boutiques."
- Discount stores often offer quality name brand merchandise at great savings, although it doesn't need to be name brand to be a quality item.
- Be a handyman. I often pick up outdoor furniture such as benches, and tables, fix them up, paint them and enjoy them. Learn how to do repairs around the house. Some of our neighbors have dubbed me the "neighborhood

handyman" because they often pay me to do work around their homes. If you have the expertise and necessary tools, you may want to work on your own cars and save a lot on labor and parts, which, by the way, are almost double at a dealership or service shop, as they not only charge for labor but also inflate the price for parts and oil. However, now-a—days, with all the new hi-tech cars, a lot of the work is simply not feasible without the proper tools and expertise.

- Other recycling is a variation of "boutique" shopping, and also has its good points. Mostly because you don't have to pay for it! I have built storage sheds, gun cabinets and various projects with supplies I've found on the sidewalk waiting for the trash collectors.
- Check out your refrigerator and pantry or cupboards then make a list of everything you need for the trip to the grocery store. Then save the receipt for the next week. Next week as you take another inventory, make note of how much unused food you throw away that you just bought the week before!

Author's Note: We must learn the difference between stocking up and hoarding.

A Few Biblical Financial Principles

It has been estimated that there are over eight hundred Scriptures in the Bible that deal with finances. I have listed only a few.

- Principle: Malachi 3:8-12 Tithes and offerings: Don't rob God, pay your tithes and offerings.
- Principle: Romans 13:8 "Owe no man anything, but to love one another: for he that loveth another hath fulfilled the law."
- Principle: Proverbs 22:7 "The rich ruleth over the poor, and the borrower is slave to the lender."
  If you default on a loan you are still obligated to repay the balance.

- Principle: Proverbs16:11; 20:10 "A just weight and balance are the Lord's: all the weights of the bag are his works. Diverse weights, and diverse measures, both of them are alike abomination to the Lord." Make sure all your business is conducted with the utmost of integrity and honesty.
- Principle: Proverbs 6:1 "My son, if thou hast stricken thy hand with a stranger, thou art snared with the words of thy mouth. Do this my son, and deliver thyself, when thou art come into the hand of thy friend; go, humble thyself, and make sure thy friend."

No Co-signing (surety): A few things to know before co-signing:

- If the debtor defaults? You are stuck with the tab.
- If the debtor makes late payments, it reflects on your credit score/rating.
- You never have ownership if the debtor defaults
- To be relieved of the liability, one must pay the debt with interest.

Definition: Surety: a promise to assume responsibility for the debt of a borrower if the borrower defaults.

I've heard of several who've lost everything because they co-signed for someone and the person defaulted. One former pastor co-signed for a close relative, who defaulted. As a result, the pastor lost his retirement, home and everything. Protect yourself!

- Principle: Proverbs 6:6-11; 30:25 "Go to the ant, thou sluggard; consider her ways, and be wise: which have no guide, overseer, or ruler, provideth her meat in the summer, and gathereth her food in the harvest. How long wilt thou sleep thou sluggard? When wilt thou arise out of thy sleep? Yet a little sleep, a little folding of the hands to sleep: so shall thy poverty come as one that travelleth, and thy want as an armed man. 30:25 The ants

are a people not strong, yet they prepare their meat in the summer."
Save for the future to avoid poverty.

- Principle: Proverbs 31:10-31 "Who can find a virtuous woman? For her price is far above rubies The heart of her husband doth safely trust in her, so that he shall have no need of spoil. She will do him good and not evil all the days of her life. She seeketh wool and flax, and worketh willingly with her hands. She is like the merchants ships; she bringeth her food from afar. She riseth also while it is yet night, and giveth meat to her household, and a portion to her maidens. She considereth a field, and buyeth it: with the fruit of her hands she planteth a vineyard. She girdeth her loins with strength, and strengtheneth her arms. She perceiveth that her merchandise is good: her candle goeth not out by night. She layeth her hands to the spindle, and her hands hold the distaff. She stretcheth out her hand to the poor; yea, she reacheth forth her hands to the needy. She is not afraid of the snow for her household: for all her household are clothed with scarlet. She maketh herself coverings of tapestry; her clothing is silk and purple. Her husband is known in the gates, when he sitteth among the elders of the land. She maketh fine linen, and selleth it; and delivereth girdles unto the merchant. Strength and honor are her clothing; and she shall rejoice in time to come. She openeth her mouth with wisdom. And in her tongue is the law of kindness. She looketh well to the ways of her household, and eateth not the bread of idleness. Her children rise up and call her blessed; her husband also, and he praiseth her. Many daughters have done virtuously, but thou excellest them all. Favor is deceitful, and beauty is vain: but a woman that feareth the Lord, she shall be praised. Give her the fruit of her hands; let her own works praise her in the gates."

Author's Note: While Proverbs 31:10-31 most definitely refers to the female gender, it can also apply to the masculine gender, simply by transposing the gender designations from female to masculine. Try it! The outcome will surprise you.

- Principle: Ecclesiastes 11:1-2 "Cast thy bread upon the waters and thou shalt find it after many days. Give a portion to seven, and also to eight; for thou knowest not what evil shall be upon the earth." Generosity, rather than selfishness, is the lesson here.
- Principle: Exodus 20:1-6 "Thou shalt have no other gods before me." Is money or material wealth your god? Self-explanatory!

Principle: Exodus 20:9-10 "Six days shalt thou labor, and do all thy work (10) but the seventh day is the Sabbath of the Lord thy God: in it thou shalt not do any work, nor thy son, not thy daughter, thy manservant, nor thy maidservant, nor thy cattle, nor thy stranger that is within thy gates." Work and labor are the concepts of prosperity, not slothfulness or laziness. The fact is that if you violate any one of these or other principles, you will not prosper. Oh, you may make a whole lot of money, but you will never prosper!

Let's Get Started

Tools required: Study Bible with concordance, "Starter Concordance of Biblical Principals," lesson 4: "Hearing God's Voice," and lesson 3: "Nine Step Biblical Process of Decision-Making."

Remember, God speaks through, and in harmony with, His written Word.

Acknowledging God

1. Pray and ask God for wisdom to solve your financial problems. Remember to acknowledge Him, literally, every step of the way from the start.

2. Find and list at least ten passages that have to deal with finances.

3. Circle the ones that most closely address your problem.

4. Be specific in identifying your particular problem. For example, if are you in debt, is your problem a lack of money, or do you need to learn how to better manage your money? Are you paying your tithes and offerings, or withholding them? You may need help in defining and clarifying.

5. If your problem is an issue with tithes and offerings, then research and study as many passages as you can find that deal with the paying of tithes and offerings.

6. If you are a committed tithe and offering giver, then research and study other financial passages for understanding of financial principles (remember it has been estimated that there are approximately eight hundred passages that deal with finances). Write the financial principles down.

7. Seek wise counsel. List at least ten mature persons from family members or close friends to help brainstorm your problem. Be sure to include some trusted professionals with expertise in the area closest to your problem. For example, list those professionals from whom you seek counsel for a mortgage, either a refinance or first mortgage, or perhaps the purchase of a car.

8. List at least ten resources on the topics of general finances, mortgages, tithes etc., including the library and Internet. Include definitions or words and terms. Better to swallow your pride and ego by asking critical questions before you sign on the dotted line. Remember, those are signed, legal documents, which will be upheld in a court of law.

9. Sort through all the information, and discard that which is not material to your problem.

10. List at least ten critical questions that require answers before a decision is made. Ask for help with this list. Remember, they are called *critical* because your future literally depends on the answers you get from those questions. Where you are tomorrow depends on the decisions you make today.

11. List all the consequences you can think of, both pro and con. See the "Column Method," Lesson 2. Remember, some may have short-term positives with long-term negative consequences, while others may be reversed. For example, many homebuyers opt for short-term positive consequences of adjustable rate mortgages with long-term negative consequences.

12. Ask yourself if you are willing to live with the potential consequences, good or bad.

13. Read and reread all information and be sure to get a clear understanding before you sign the contract. That includes defining and understanding any and all terms and contract language. Acquire definitions of all terms, see internet, under mortgage terms.

Sample Critical Mortgage Questions

You will need the correct answers to avert financial chaos.

1. How long do I/we expect to live in this home?
2. What is the interest note rate?
3. What is the APR? (annual percentage rate)
4. What does the APR mean and include?
5. Why is the APR higher than the note rate?
6. How much will this loan cost in dollars and cents?
7. When will my/our home be paid off?

8. Can I/we afford this payment, or is it too high for our budget?
9. Is this the right size house for us, or should we downsize or upsize?
10. What does POC mean?
11. What does buy down mean?
12. What does it mean to pay points?

The following questions may not avert financial chaos, nonetheless, they are vital.

1. What is the neighborhood like?
2. Are there schools nearby?
3. What are the neighbors like?

Samples of Financial Information Sources

- ➤ AARP magazines
- ➤ Consumer Report Magazine
- ➤ Consumer Credit Counseling Service
- ➤ Credit Unions (many have online calculators)
- ➤ Family Circle Magazine has financial tips from time to time
- ➤ Money Magazine
- ➤ Networking with older and younger generations
- ➤ Woman's Day Magazine (selected articles)
- ➤ Jane Bryant Quinn's financial column

Retirement

Sample of Critical Questions

1. What Biblical principles apply to my retirement years?
2. At what age should I begin thinking about retirement?
3. At what age should I begin planning and saving for retirement?
4. At what age do I want to retire?
5. At what age can I retire, if possible to determine?

6. Approximately how much money will I need for retirement?
7. Where will I live out my retirement years? City, state etc.
8. What types of investments are best suited for me?
9. How long do I anticipate my money will last?
10. What biblical principles, if any, apply to my situation?
11. Will I have Social Security?
12. Will I need supplemental medical insurance?
13. Who do I know that is retired and can give me insight?
14. Do I have enough for health care? Dental? Final expenses?
15. Will my mortgage be paid off before I retire?
16. Will my financial resources support my prospective lifestyle?
17. Will I need to keep on working? If so, how long?
18. Will I be close to immediate family members, physically, emotionally?
19. Is my estate in order?
20. How do I determine if I need an attorney?
21. What are the costs of living in various prospective places?
22. Will I need to live with my adult children? If so, which one?
23. Will I live in assisted living or in my own home?
24. At what age should I stop thinking about and planning for retirement? (Retirement thinking and planning should never stop, as situations are continually changing.)

Faith Building Practice and Review

1. Review the section on stewardship. Which kind of steward are you?

2. How many red flags are you ignoring?

3. If you are still ignoring the red flags, but just can't seem to help yourself, then pray for the Lord's help to overcome

these areas. You may need to have outside professional counseling.

4. Review the "Financial Patterns" section and list both the negative and positive ones that you are practicing. See "Column Method," lesson 2.

5. List some other "frugal tips."

6. Are you a tithe payer?

7. Why or why not?

8. Are you guilty of hiding your tithe with your own "stuff" (see Josh.7:1-11)?

9. Discuss why it is so important to be a tithe payer.

10. Review and discuss the sample mortgage and retirement questions.

11. What do the Scriptures say about co-signing? See Prov. 6:1-5; 11:15; 24:30; 24:31; 26:13.

12. How are we to free ourselves from co-signing for someone Prov. 6:3-5?

Notes

Notes

Lesson 8

Marriage and Relationships

Most of us are not instructed in the fine art of selecting a lifelong mate of how to select good friends. This lesson should be of help in this vital area of our lives.

For this lesson you will need to review lesson 3: "Nine Step Biblical Process of Decision-Making."

1) Acknowledge the Lord (every step of the way)
   - Pray
   - Look for biblical principles
   - Listen to His voice

2) Ascertain what information is needed
   - Much will be determined by the biblical principles you discover.
   - Where do I look for a potential spouse?
   - Where should I not look for a potential spouse?
   - For whom do I look?
   - What are my *needs* in a spouse?
   - What are my potential spouse's needs in me?

3) Analyze the information (including relevant Scriptures)
   - Do I really understand what I'm getting into?
   - Is this someone I really want to be with?

4) Weigh the consequences, whether good or bad

5) Seek wisdom and advice (possible resources)
   - Friends
   - Relatives
   - Pastor
   - Church members

6) What biblical principles might be violated?

Principle: 2Corinthians 6:14-15 "Be ye not unequally together with unbelievers: for what fellowship hath righteousness with unrighteousness? And what communion hath light with darkness? And what concord hath Christ with Belial? Or what part hath he that believeth with an infidel?"

Author's Note: one of the greatest mistakes a Christian can make is to become bound together in marriage or into a business relationship with an unbeliever. Their values and belief systems are not alike. The Scriptures, most often, show the believer succumbing to the ways of the unbeliever.

Principle: Proverbs 22:24-25 "Make no friendship with an angry man and with a furious man thou shalt not go: lest thou learn his ways and get a snare to thy soul." While many unbelievers display many Christian virtues, their fundamental belief system is flawed. Trust, respect, and integrity are often sacrificed for the relationship.

7) Discard irrelevant information
   - Rumors (unless substantiated)

8) Decide which is the best solution:
   - Go ahead with relationship
   - Cut off the relationship

9) Implement the solution

Inner or Hidden Man of the Heart versus the Outer Package

Principle: 1Peter 3:1-4 "Likewise, ye wives, be in subjection to your own husbands; that, if any obey not the word, they may also without the word be won by the chaste conversation of the wives; while they behold your chaste conversation, coupled with fear. Whose adorning let it not be that outward adorning of the plaiting of the hair, and of wearing of gold, or the putting on of apparel; but let it be the hidden man of the heart, in that which is not corruptible, even the ornament of a meek and quiet spirit, which in the sight of God is of great price." (A *chaste conversation* is a disciplined lifestyle.)

So what is the "hidden man of the heart"? Consider this partial list:

- Mutual beliefs (Scriptures place this as the #1 point to look for 2 Cor. 6:14-18)
- Trust
- Faithfulness
- Love
- Humility
- Integrity
- Loyalty
- Compassion
- Gentleness
- Meekness
- Forgiveness
- Temperance, self-control
- Mutual commitment
- Mutual respect

These are qualities you should possess and maintain and look for in seeking a relationship of any kind, whether for marriage or friendship. They should reflect your core values and beliefs.

Author's Note: Simply put, your core values should be the same as your principles!

How Do I Find the Right Person to Befriend or Marry?

Rephrasing the question: what qualities or virtues should I be looking for in a friend or partner in marriage?

Consider interacting with the person you want to get to know, with people you really respect. Many times the feelings or messages you receive from those closest to you are correct, as they have your best interests at heart, whereas your candidate is more likely to have his or her own interests elevated above yours.

- Always be in prayer.
- Look at your own relationship with God and those closest to you, such as your parents and siblings.
- Have your life as together as possible (no one is perfect) in terms of employment, finances, health, insurance, etc. Your life doesn't have to be perfect with God, but it should show that you follow Godly principles.
- Meet people with the idea of becoming an acquaintance. Even if you think a person may make a good companion—take it slow and easy. Spend time getting to know him or her before you "fall in love."
- Observe how your prospect interacts with others in a group setting, such as a church outing or function.
- Observe the person's family and how they relate to one another. A controlling and manipulative mother or father will quite often produce controlling and manipulative offspring. Do they have good conflict management skills? Can you live with that?
- Be observant as to how ex-wives and ex-husbands treat each other.

- Listen and watch for "red flags" such as lying, and "things just not adding up." Quirky ideas may well turn out to be vicious vices with your beloved.
- Do you manifest the fruit of the Spirit (Ga.5:22-26)?
- Does your prospect manifest the fruit of the Spirit?
- Does your prospect have good conflict management skills? Do you?
- Discover your core needs (they are common to most everyone).
- Discover the other person's core needs.
- Ask yourself: Am I able and willing to fulfill the needs of this person? Are they able and willing to fulfill my needs?
- What work ethic does your person of interest have? Work ethic may speak volumes about their character. As you read Prov.31:10-31, remember that the virtues mentioned may apply to both male and female, even though the chapter is written concerning a woman.
- Ask them to pull a credit report for you the review.

Core needs

Affection, recreational companionship, security, sexual fulfillment, conversation, domestic support, intimacy, commitment, admiration, honesty, openness, spiritual leadership, attractiveness, tenderness, understanding, compassion

Marital Myths

I'll just change him or her.

- There is the misconception that says, "I know he or she is not perfect but I'll change him."
- Ever heard that one?
- Ever used it?
- Does it or did it work?

If you become connected with someone with different core values and beliefs and try to keep that person, you quickly will become frustrated, and *your* behavior and manners will change ever so subtly, instead of theirs.

Does age matter?

Age does matter:

- Just a ten year gap in age can mean the difference in thinking about retirement. Often the younger person isn't as concerned with retirement until later in the relationship, while the elder of the couple is inundated with anxiety about retirement and can't understand why their spouse seems unconcerned. The same thing may apply to having children. Procreation may be a point of potential conflict as the elder of the couple may have lost the interest in raising children. Can you imagine what a twenty, thirty or perhaps forty year age gap can mean?
- Health issues can arise at any age. However, generally speaking, the older a person becomes, more serious issues are likely to arise.
- Maturity may also be a major area of conflict as the age gap widens. The more mature person often thinks differently on major and minor issues.

We're so much in love.

- We're so much in love we'll always get along together.
- If you're so much in love, there will never be any arguments or problems.
- We're perfect for each other.

High Maintenance

- Emotionally: the high maintenance person lives life on the edge of frayed emotions, often wearing their feelings on their sleeves, becoming burdensome for others.

- Materialistically: the materialistic person seems to have an unquenchable thirst for material goods. This person can literally destroy a family budget.
- Mentally: may suffer from a number of mental deficiencies with numerous causes.
- Physically: may be physically handicapped in one or more ways.
- Spiritually: never able to feed themselves on the Word of God; always "spiritual babies," never reaching or striving for spiritual maturity. Heb.5:11-14

Unequally Yoked

Principle: 2Corinthians 6:14-18 "Be ye not unequally yoked together with unbelievers: for what fellowship hath righteousness with unrighteousness? And what communion hath light with darkness? And what concord hath Christ with Belial? Or what part hath he with an infidel? And what agreement hath the temple of God with idols? For ye are the temple of the living God; as God hath said I will dwell in them and walk in them; and I will be their God and they shall be my people. Wherefore come out from among them, and be ye separate, saith the Lord, and touch not the unclean thing; and I will receive you, and will be a Father unto you, and ye shall be my sons and daughters, saith the Lord Almighty."

The key term is *infidel*, which means "unbeliever"; literally, one without faith.

Principle: Genesis 24:3 "And I will make thee swear by the Lord, the God of heaven, and the God of the earth, that thou shalt not take a wife unto my son of the daughters of the Canaanites, among whom I dwell: but thou shalt go unto my country, and to my kindred, and take a wife unto my son Isaac."

Abraham knew and instructed his servant not to bring a Canaanite woman, unbeliever, to be wed to his son. Samson's consequence with Delilah, the Philistine woman, was losing his eyesight, strength, and eventually his life.

Definition:

Yoking is a term used by farmers when plowing a field with a pair of oxen. The two animals are joined together by means of a wooden yoke placed around their necks and a harness about the head. They have to be of fairly equal size, temperament and strength, and would have to have a mind to work together, or else they would be nothing but trouble. Often a younger ox was paired with a mature ox to learn to pull properly.

Solomon's Example

God told Israel not to multiply wives unto themselves, for in so doing, they (the wives), would change the hearts of the children of Israel. Solomon, in all his wisdom, had seven hundred wives and three hundred concubines, mostly from nations other that Israel. Solomon often married from other nations to effect a peace arrangement between Israel and the warring nations, and they turned his heart from the Lord, eventually dividing the kingdom. (1Kings 11:1-6) Although we have no scriptural evidence that Solomon had sexual intimacy with all of these women, the fact remains that he took them as his wives, thus violating the commandment of God.

Author's Note: Turning your heart from God need not take as many wives as Solomon. It takes only one nonbeliever to turn your heart from the Lord. It's a Biblical principle. See Deut.17:17; 2Cor.6:14.

Cursed vs. Blessed

The thrust of the principle in 2Cor.6:14-18 is toward being yoked together with unbelievers, and *not* the quantity.

Principle: Deuteronomy 17:17a "Neither shall he multiply wives unto himself, that his heart turn not away:"

This Old Testament passage does not mention being married to an unbeliever. Rather, it infers that the taking of more than one wife, either believer or unbeliever, will turn the heart away from God.

Adultery

Principle: Proverbs 6:27-29, 32-33; Exodus20:14; Leviticus20:10 "Can a man take fire into his bosom and his clothes not be burned? Can one go upon hot coals, and his feet not be burned? So he that goeth into his neighbor's wife; whosoever toucheth her shall not be innocent. But whoso committeth adultery with a woman lacketh understanding: he that doeth it destroyeth his own soul. A wound and dishonor shall he get; and his reproach shall not be wiped away."

Definition:

Adultery is generally defined as an extramarital affair with a married person. Fornication is generally defined as any other sexual perversion of intimacy, such as incest, or bestiality, or sexual intimacy between two unmarried individuals. Same sex relations are also in the category of fornication.

Married for All the Wrong Reasons

Here is a partial list of wrong reasons for getting married:

* To get away from parents
* Loneliness
* Adventure and excitement
* All my friends are married
* Sex (great in bed)
* He or she has a terrific body

Divorce

Paul told the Church at Corinth, 1Cor.7:10-16, that a believing spouse ought not to leave an unbelieving spouse, because the believer sanctifies the unbeliever. That does not, however, give license to purposefully marry an unbeliever and ignore and rebel against the Scriptures.

Rather, Paul was addressing a problem within the church at Corinth, namely that the couple was already united in marriage before either of them became born-again, and that sometime afterward, one of them accepted Christ as Savior. Then the circumstance changed, as one became a follower of Christ, while the other remained unsaved. Therefore Paul instructed that the couple should remain together unless the unbeliever desired to leave or divorce. It was not an authorization for a believer to marry an unbeliever!

Principle: Mark 10:2-9 "And the Pharisees came to him, and asked him, "Is it lawful for a man to put away his wife?" tempting him. And he answered and said unto them, What did Moses command you? And they said, Moses suffered to write a bill of divorcement, and to put her away. And Jesus answered and said unto them, For the hardness of your heart he wrote you this precept. But from the beginning of the creation God made them male and female. For this cause shall a man leave his father and mother, and cleave to his wife; and they twain shall be one flesh: so then they are no more twain, but one flesh. What therefore God hath joined together, let not man put asunder."

Matt. 19:8 "He saith unto them, Moses because of your hardness of heart suffered you to put away your wives: but from the beginning it was not so."

Think carefully about the commandments and implications against divorce. In most cases I believe it would be far better to work out the differences through Christian counseling, especially where there are young children involved. Be careful that your heart does not harden. God takes marriage and divorce seriously, contrary to contemporary society, which has a tendency to take divorce and marriage too lightly.

Survey of Reasons for Attraction (2007)

In 2007, I sent a survey to several of my closest friends and relatives, to which fourteen men and women responded. One survey question asked the reason for attraction to their spouse. Their responses varied, and included the following reasons:

- Warmth
- Humor
- Charisma
- Kindness
- Consideration
- Physical attraction (physique)
- Love at first sight
- Wit
- Intelligence
- Hygiene
- Wealth
- Athletic ability
- Hormones

Recommended Reading

1) *His Needs Her Needs* by Willard Harley Jr. ISBN 008007-1788-0
2) *Before Love Dies* by Larry J. Russell M.A. ISBN-10 1880809931
3) Radio Bible Class booklets (RBC) (may be ordered free from RBC)
   a. How Can I Know Who To Marry?
   b. What Does God Expect of a Man: masculine role?
   c. What Does God Expect of Woman: feminine role?
   d. How Can We Avoid the Lure of Sexual Sin?
   e. Divorce & Remarriage?
   f. What is the Promise of Marriage?

    g. What Will Make My Marriage Work?

    h. What Is Real Love?

    i.   God's Protection of Women

Faith Building Practice and Review

1. What character traits are you looking for in a friend?

2. What character traits are you looking for in a spouse?

3. How do those traits compare to the biblical traits?

4. From the Scriptures, list three bad character traits and the reasons to avoid them. For example: anger problems, Povr. 22:24

5. Make a list of trusted, mature friends and relatives who would aid you in the process of selecting meaningful relationships.

6. Observe the qualities of other persons, and determine whether or not they would be suitable for you.

7. Be especially prayerful that God will make you the person you need to be.

8. Are you high maintenance? If need be, have a professional counselor help you identify your specific high maintenance

area. The idea is to bring you help, comfort, aid, and assistance, not to belittle or embarrass you.

9. If so, pray and ask God to deliver you from high maintenance.

10. Remember, no one is perfect. Neither are you, so don't be hypercritical.

11. Are you currently contemplating a relationship with an unbeliever?

12. If so, how do you justify that relationship with the Word of God?

13. Explain the benefits of having good conflict resolution skills.

14. Discuss the pros and cons of the age gap using various age increments such as ten, twenty, and thirty years.

15. List and discuss any other marital myths you can think of.

16. Discuss work ethic and how it affects a person's character.

17. Discuss the differences, if any, between principles and core values.

18. Make a list of your personal principles/core values and prioritize them.

Notes

Notes

Lesson 9

Reversing the Curse

Principle: 2Chronicles 7:14 "If my people, which are called by my name, shall humble themselves, and pray, and seek my face, and turn from their wicked ways; then I will hear from heaven, and will forgive their sin, and will heal their land."

It is grossly unfair and cruel to pronounce a disease without leaving the prescription for the cure. Throughout Scripture, God has always warned his people of the consequences of sin and bad decisions. However, He always presented the cure. It makes no difference if it is outright sin, or a matter of bad business decisions. The cure is 2 Chron.7:14.

King David numbered the children of Israel against the command of God and thousands were killed by the plague! However, as soon as David acknowledged his sin and confessed it, the plague was stayed. 2 Sam. 24:1-25

So, how does that relate to, say, bad financial or relationship decisions? The passages above set four rules to remedy the situation.

1) Humble yourself. Let go of your pride (1 Peter5:6).
2) Pray. Ask for divine intervention and guidance, which will be manifest in the next step.
3) Seek God's face. In other words, seek wisdom and wise counsel.

4) Repent. Turn from what you're doing, to what the newly found wisdom and counsel show you.

After you have sincerely completed the steps above, then, and only then, will God begin to move on your behalf! In His own time He will heal your finances, relationships, heart, mind, soul, and body.

Review the chapters in this book and get familiar with the principles outlined, and learn the processes for prudent decision-making.

Remember, the consequences will not change for our ill judgments, but if we will take the time to learn and practice the principles in *Crossroads of Life,* we can begin to reverse the curses in our lives. For instance:

- An adulterous affair may end your marriage, but if you repent and learn the principles of good relationships, then selecting a soul mate for your next marriage will make that marriage be blessed instead of cursed.
- You may have wreaked havoc with your finances, but if you learn sound biblical principles, you can turn your finances into blessings.
- You may have been fired from every job you've ever had, but if you apply the principles of integrity and honesty, work hard, and seek your strong points, you can turn your work history around.

Author's Note: God's way is to repent, not to pray for a fire escape, only to run back into the fire later on, or to set another fire! As I said earlier, God's Word has never been intended to be used as a fire escape. It is intended to stop you from setting fires in the first place! That, my friend, is success and prosperity!

You Can't Change the Past

A common misconception is that you can reverse the consequences of your actions by simply confessing. Nothing could be further from the truth! Repentance is different from confession in that repentance involves a one-hundred-and-eighty degree change of direction, whereas confession, in general, is an acceptance of ownership without a change of direction.

For example; When King David numbered the children of Israel against God's will, there was a great plague that took the lives of thousands of God's people. However, when David repented that he had numbered the people, those lost to the plague did not return to life and go on as if nothing had happened!

Principle: 2Samuel 24:10, 15, 17 And David's heart smote him after that he had numbered the people. And David said unto the Lord I have sinned greatly in that I have done: and now I beseech thee, O Lord, take away the iniquity of thy servant; for I have done very foolishly. So the Lord sent a pestilence upon Israel from the morning even to the time appointed: and there died of the people of Dan even to Beersheba seventy thousand men. And David spoke unto the angel of the Lord when he saw the angel that smote the people, and said, Lo, I have sinned wickedly: but these sheep, what have they done? Let thine hand, I pray thee, be against me and against my father's house.

The reason David was called a man after God's heart was that he always sought God's forgiveness after sinning, and took responsibility for his actions.

Author's Note: A person's past behavior usually determines their future behavior.

Sowing and Reaping

Principle: Galatians 6:7 "Be not deceived; God is not mocked: for whatsoever a man soweth, that shall he also reap."

There is a saying that, "What goes around, comes around"; in other words if you live by lies and deceit, lies and deceit will eventually destroy you.

Sin produces sin and sin brings destruction. Righteousness produces righteousness.

Principle: Genesis 1:24-26 "And God said, Let the earth bring forth the living creature after his kind, cattle and creeping thing, and beast of the earth after his kind: and it was so. and God made the beast of the earth after his kind, and the cattle after their kind, and everything that creepeth upon the earth after his kind: and Gods saw that it was good. and God said, Let us make man in our image, after our likeness: and let them have dominion over the fish of the sea, and over the fowl of the air, and over the cattle, and over all the earth, and over every creeping thing that creepeth upon the earth."

Crop Failure

In times past, I used to hear the phrase "praying for crop failure," meaning that after you'd committed a wrong, you would then commence to pray that the wrong you committed would somehow turn out to be the right thing. Personally, I don't know if it works or not. I prefer to use the method of sowing and reaping. I don't see the value in praying for something if you don't intend to change your way of doing things.

If you are tired of having the same results time after time, then it's time to make some changes in the way you make decisions. 2 Chron. 7:14 is the answer to all your problems!

Faith Building Practice and Review

1. Have you ever done or said something you later regretted?

2. Did God somehow "reverse" the wrong as if it never happened?

3. Discuss how this lesson applies to making decisions that are not necessarily morally wrong.

4. Have you ever made a bad financial decision that cost you a lot of money?

5. Did you get the money back after you repented?

6. When is the last time you jumped out of an aircraft without a parachute?

7. How did it turn out?

8. Do you know of anyone who had children out of wedlock?

9. What happened to those children after the person repented and got married?

Notes

Lesson 10

Where Should I Worship?

By following the outline in lesson 3: "Nine Step Biblical Process," one can find his or her place of worship. It is imperative to know that you are in the church family that God has chosen for you for that particular season of your life. By that I mean we are to grow "from faith to faith" (Rom. 1:17), just as in the natural way we grow from elementary school, to middle school, to high school, to college, and never stop growing and learning throughout our lives. So, also, God may sometimes move you to a higher level of faith by moving you to another church family.

However, it is unwise to keep jumping from one church to another without God's guidance.

Principle: Psalm 68:6 God setteth the solitary in families: he bringeth out those which are bound with chains: but the rebellious dwell in a dry land.

God knows that being in a good church home and environment is conducive to producing mature children for Him.

Principle: Hebrews 10:25 "Not forsaking the assembling of ourselves together as the manner of some is; but exhorting one another: and so much more, as ye see the day approaching."

If you want to stunt your physical growth, abstain from food and see how long you survive. You will never be a mature, fruit-producing child of God if you neglect worship and fellowship with other believers. In order not to stunt your spiritual (and emotional) growth, you need feed yourself on the Word of God.

Finding the right place to worship is vital to the spiritual health of every believer, and yet there seems to be so little to guide us. In times past, I have told people to go where they are being fed the Word and growing, and I still believe it to be true.

However, the question becomes: How do I know the Word is being taught?

I believe the answer is that, unless you are a student of the Word yourself, you really will not know if it truly is the Word of God, but that does not mean you have to go to Bible college or seminary to learn the Bible.

For example: just because someone quotes Scripture does not necessarily mean it is God's Word. What if that person takes Scripture out of context or misuses the Scriptures and twists them to say what he or she wants them to say? Is that the Word of God? I dare say a resounding NO! That is why each believer needs to diligently study the Scriptures for themselves.

Principle: Acts17:11b "who searched the Scriptures daily, whether those things were so."

Of necessity we ought to be as the church in Berea, continually searching the Scriptures daily, to affirm the truth and expose error.

In Hebrews 5:12-14 Paul admonishes the church to grow-up that it might be able to discern both good and evil.

1. Acknowledge the Lord
   - Pray
   - Follow biblical principles
   - Listen to His voice

2. What information is needed
   - Which denomination?
   - What do they teach and practice?
   - Are there any "perfect" churches?
   - Visit several churches, several times
   - Speak with the pastor(s) and members
   - Are they Bible based?
   - Do they practice agape love?

3. Analyze the information
   - Do you really understand their doctrine, mission, and purpose?

4. Seek wisdom and advice
   - What do friends and relatives think?

5. What Biblical principles might be openly violated?
6. Are there any red flags?
7. Discard irrelevant information.
8. Seek the best solution. If more than one church is in consideration you may have to discern the best for you by repeating steps 1-7.
9. Implement the solution (join or find another one)

The Purpose of the Church

a. To perfect the saints/believers for the work of the ministry (Eph.4:12)
b. To bring unity in the faith, maturity (Eph.4:14)
c. To evangelize souls; promote fellowship, praise and worship (Acts 2:37-47)
d. To care for widows, the fatherless and orphans (Ats. 6:1)
e. To rightly divide/discern the Word of truth (2Tim. 2:15)
f. To provide sound doctrine (2 Tim. 4:3)
g. To feed the flock (Psalm 23:2; John 21:15, 16, 17) [A healthy church is a well fed church] with both natural and spiritual food
h. To exhort people to godly living (Heb. 10:25)

The Purpose of Church Membership

Principle: Psalm 68:6 "God setteth the solitary in families: he bringeth out those which are bound in chains: but the rebellious dwell in a dry land." We all need fellowship with other believers in order to grow.

Principle: Psalm 92:13-15 "Those that be planted in the house of the Lord shall flourish in the courts of our God. They shall bring forth fruit in old age; they shall be fat and flourishing; to shew that the Lord is upright: he is my rock, and there is no unrighteousness in him."

In order to flourish spiritually, it is important to be planted in a church family, socially and emotionally.

Numerous passages indicate that it is the Lord God who draws us out of the bondage of slavery to sin, and not we ourselves. See John 6:44; John 12:32; Jer.31. after He draws us out, He places, or plants, us in church families for the purpose of flourishing and worshipping Him.

"Planting" means that we are to become members of that church, and as members we are to flourish by becoming active in worship, song, education and Bible study. See John15:1-8. Production and flourishing do not come by "pew warming." They come by setting your roots firmly in the ground, and growing and working together with the other members.

It is impossible for a plant to flourish without its roots being planted in fertile soil, thus becoming a "member" of the soil. So, also, we are joined in the fertile soil of the church where God has planted us we set our roots in membership and find a place to serve.

How not to look for a Church

Some people seek out churches for all the wrong reasons. However, what they want and what they need are often not the same things. Here is a partial list:

- The "meat market approach": some check out the "chicks or babes," or the "hunks and beefcakes," or even the "cute Pastor," to see what might be available.
- Business: some are there to make business connections to line up the "big deal."
- Entertainment: they only go for the Christmas and Easter services and plays, or when a big name celebrity singer is town.
- Idol worship: That Pastor sure can preach!
- Friendship: All my friends go there.
- Tradition: all my ancestors went or go there. They built the church.
- Convenience: It's handy or close by.
- Aesthetics: It's a beautiful building.

Brick and Mortar

In 1Chronicles 22, David had stockpiled the building materials for the temple of God. There was nothing but the finest of cedar wood from Lebanon, skilled craftsmen and masons, the finest of gold, silver, brass, etcetera. Likewise, the tabernacle in the wilderness was built with the finest of materials. However, all the building materials were not to be used as a pattern for a place of worship. Rather, those supplies were an outward type and shadow of the inward beauty of the heart! God built the very place of worship in heart of man, out of none other than mud. Read it in Genesis 2.

Don't get caught up in the outward tapestries of stained glass windows, elaborate carpet, etc. Rather, focus on the inward things of the heart.

In John 4, at the well, Jesus told the Samaritan woman, that the true worshippers would worship God in spirit and truth, not giving mention of either geographic location or unique and ornate fixtures.

Throughout the New Testament, the emphasis is on the inward purity of the heart and not the outward appearance of either the person or the edifice.

When we focus on the wrong thing, such as outward appearance, our values become distorted and hazy, and our worship can become methodical, lackadaisical and mundane. Therefore, our worship is unacceptable to God.

A second purpose of the brick-and-mortar illustration is found in Eph. 4:16, "from whom the whole body fitly joined together and compacted by that which every joint supplied, according to the effectual working in the measure of every part, maketh increase of the body unto the edifying of itself in love."

Simply stated, it is essential for the entire body to function as Christ would direct.

> 1 Corinthians12:12-18 "For as the body is one, and hath many members, and all the members of that one body, being many are one: so also is Christ. For by one Spirit are we baptized into one body, whether we be Jews or Gentiles, whether we be bond or free; and have all been made to drink into one Spirit. For the body is not one member, but many. if the foot shall say, because I am not the hand, I am not of the body; is it therefore not of the body? And if the ear shall say, because I am not the eye, I am not of the body; is it therefore not of the body? If the whole body were an eye, where the hearing? If the whole were hearing, where were the smelling? But now hath God set the members every one of them in the body as it hath pleased him."

Author's Note: the emphasis here is that although the function of some members appear to pale compared to others, yet all are vital, as a whole, to the corporate body.

Some say church membership or attendance is unimportant and unnecessary, however God says different. God says that everyone is of equal importance to the functioning of the entire body, no matter how small or insignificant each may seem. Read and study 1Cor. 12:15-31.

The Pastor's Heart

Principle: Jeremiah 3:15 "And I will give you pastors according to mine own heart, which shall feed you with knowledge and understanding." God's pastors should have the heart of God to properly feed and nourish you.

Principle: John 21:15-17 "Feed my sheep." Jesus instructed Peter three times to "feed my sheep" in these three verses. It is a direct command to ministers to make sure they are feeding God's people the Word of God.

Principle: John 10:11-15 "lay down life for sheep." This speaks of the unselfish life that God's pastors should have.

Principle: Psalm 23:1-6 is not only a description of Christ as our Shepherd, but also is a pattern for contemporary shepherds/pastors.

- God's heart
- Feeds with knowledge and understanding
- Protects
- Provides
- Leads by example

Author's Note: whatever the pastor's heart is will filter down through the staff, and will eventually permeate the entire flock.

If the pastor has a heart for missions, it will eventually filter down to the flock. If the pastor has a heart for prison ministry, the church will be focused on ministry in prisons. Likewise if the pastor is not well studied and prepared it will show in the congregation. If the pastor is engaged in adultery, sinful activities, or is a hard taskmaster, it will likewise permeate the entire church. Know your pastor's heart.

How Do You Know When It's Time to Leave?

Recently I was asked, "How do you know when it is time to leave a church and search for another?"

There are several answers to this vital question.

1. God may be calling you to another level at another church.

   Principle: Romans1:17 "For therein is the righteousness revealed from faith to faith: as it is written, the just shall live by faith." This means that a person's faith must be replenished and grow or it wither and die. I often say that no one can take another farther than they themselves are. In other words, I cannot teach you calculus or trigonometry if I only passed general math.

   Principle: Ephesians 5:11-13 "And he gave some apostles; and some, prophets; and some, evangelists; and some, pastors and teachers; for the perfecting of the saints, for the work of the ministry, for the edifying of the body of Christ: till we all come in the unity of the faith, and the knowledge of the Son of God, and unto a perfect man, unto the measure of the stature of the fullness of Christ." The church is to bring you to maturity for the work of the ministry. It is not a social entity.

2. Lack of spiritual growth (starving souls).
3. Lack of proper church discipline. The Scriptures state that everyone must be held accountable, from the pastor and church leaders right on down to the sheep in the pew. Why? For one reason. The church is supposed to be a shining light to the world, and if that light is obscured by sin inside, it cannot possibly illuminate the dark world we live in! The Old and New Testaments both show examples of leaders being disciplined and held accountable for their behavior.

Author's Note: If there is no self-discipline or corporate discipline, then the light of the church is put out both, corporately and individually! See Rev. 2-3

> Principle: Matthew 5:13-16 "Ye are the salt of the earth: but if the salt has lost his savor wherewith shall it be salted? It is thenceforth good for nothing, but to be cast out, and to be trodden under foot of men. Ye are the light of the world. A city that is set on a hill cannot be hid. Neither do men light a candle, and put it under a bushel, but on a candlestick; and it giveth light unto all that are in the house. Let your light so shine before men, that they may see your good works, and glorify your Father which is in heaven." An undisciplined soul is not worth its salt, nor is it light in a dark world. Rather, it brings disdain and is a reproach to the name and body of Christ.

> Principle: John 15:2 "Every branch in me that beareth not fruit he taketh away: and every branch that beareth fruit, he purgeth it, that it might bring forth more fruit." A barren fruit tree is worthless, as its sole purpose is to provide fruit to the owner.

4. Abuse: most people know the difference between discipline and abuse.

> Principle: 1Peter 5:2-3 "Feed the flock of God which is among you, taking the oversight thereof, not by constraint, but willingly, but of a ready mind; neither as being lords over God's heritage, but ensamples to the flock."
> 1 Peter 5:2-3 (Amplified Bible) "Tend (nurture, guard, guide and fold) the flock of God that is your responsibility, not by coercion or constraint but willingly; not dishonorably motivated by the [belonging to the office] but eagerly and cheerfully. Not (as arrogant, dictatorial and overbearing persons) domineering over those in your charge, but

being examples (patterns and models of Christian living) to the flock (the congregation)."

Author's Note: Anything other than Scriptural treatment of the parishioners constitutes abuse by God's standards.

In ancient times, the shepherd did not own the sheep. He watched over the sheep, which belonged to someone else. They were not his own, though he treated them as his own. David never abused his father's sheep! He cared for and loved them as his own.

5. Heresy and Doctrinal Error:

Principle: Galatians1:6-9 "I marvel that ye are so soon removed from him that called you into the grace of Christ unto another gospel: which is not another; but there be some that trouble you, and would pervert the gospel of Christ. But though we, or an angel from heaven, preach any other gospel unto you than that we have preached unto you, let him be accursed. As we said before, so say I now again, if man preach any other gospel unto you than you have received, let him be accursed."
Of course this requires that each child of God diligently study the Word of God in order to discern truth from error.

Principle: Acts 17:11 "These were more noble than those in Thessalonica, in that they received the Word with all readiness of mind, and searched the Scriptures daily, whether those things were so."
Every one ought to be like the believers in Berea, studying the Word of God daily to discern truth from error. 2Tim.2:15 is a parallel passage, whereby each believer is charged with the study of God's Word, and is thereby able to correctly discern the truth.

Spiritual Gifts

All the Spiritual gifts listed in Romans 12:4-10 and 1Corinthians12-14 are vital to the success and prosperity of any church and therefore ought to be manifest. Read and diligently study the above passages.

Faith Building Review and Practice

1. Name three things to look for when searching for a church home.

2. Name the seven purposes of the church.

3. What constitutes abuse in the church?

4. List five ways the ministers and church leaders are to treat God's people.

5. Who is subject to church discipline?

6. Who is exempt from church discipline?

7. Is God leading you to a new church home?

8. How do you know?

9. Are you a student of the Word, or a babe in Christ, needing to be fed by others? Heb. 5:12-4?

10. Are you being fed and growing where you currently attend?

11. Is your soul being blessed where you currently attend?

12. Why did you choose the place of worship you are in?

13. Do you sincerely desire to worship in spirit and truth?

14. Are you caught up in the glitter, glamour and excitement?

15. Is your worship pleasing to God or a charade before men?

16. What constitutes heresy or doctrinal error?

17. Do you search the Scriptures daily with readiness of mind to discern whether or not you are being led astray?

18. Explain the difference between discipline and abuse.

19. What is your pastor's heart?

20. Do you support your pastor's heart?

21. In what ways do you support your pastor's heart?

22. Diligently study the spiritual gifts in 1Cor.12 and in Rom. 12:4-8 and record your findings.

23. What does it mean to be "fitly joined together"?

24. Are you fitly joined together with your church?

25. List three ways are you fitly joined together with your church.

Notes

Notes

Lesson 11

Election Time

The purpose of this lesson is to impart the importance of going to the polls during elections, even if it is by absentee ballot.

At a monthly breakfast for men, the subject of an up-coming election was the topic of the morning. Questions and discussions covered the whole spectrum, from which candidate was best qualified to which issue was most important. Sometimes these kinds of discussions can become very heated and spirited, to say the least.

Every election appears to be "the most important" election in history. Or at least it's implied to be by political experts.

Every election is important, whether it's a local, state, or national election. Each election has issues and candidates to be selected by the voters, some of which will affect the lives of every citizen in this country, whether or not they choose to vote.

There are issues on health care, taxes, zoning, highway maintenance, and a myriad of other selected issues.

There are candidates running for public office; president, vice-president, senators, congressmen and women, judges, governors and so on. Each elected official has influence in the passing of laws and legislation, regulations, impose taxes, etc., which will eventually affect all of us in a variety of ways, including retirement, health care, taxes (again?), and virtually every aspect of our way of life!

That being said, let us examine a few passages of Scripture regarding the issue at hand.

Casting Lots or Voting

On the surface, casting lots and voting may appear to be the same thing, but rest assured, they are not!

Casting Lots: "In ancient times disputed questions, by most nations, were often settled by the casting of lots. Magistrates and priests were appointed by casting lots, and the land of conquered enemies was distributed by its means.

"We have no information given in Scripture concerning the mode by which lots were cast. Among the Latins, especially where several parties were concerned, 'little counters of wood', or of some other light material, were put into a jar (called *sitella*) with a neck so narrow that only one could come out at a time. After the jar had been filled with water and the contents shaken, the lots were determined by the order in which the bits of wood, representing the several parties, came out of the water."[4]

In Acts1:15-26, Justus and Matthias were candidates for the office of Apostle, recently vacated by Judas Iscariot. The lot fell upon Matthias and he was counted among the eleven other apostles, thus taking the place of Judas Iscariot.

The Roman soldiers divided the garments of Jesus by casting lots (Matt. 27:35). Casting lots is basically assigned to a select few, thereby making the decision.

Voting: voting is another avenue for making decisions. In democratic societies, voting is the accepted norm for making decisions, as well as for electing officials, selecting between

---

[4]   James M. Freeman, *Manners and Customs of the Bible*, reprinted Logos International, 1972 from original printing of Nelson and Phillips, New York, page 237. Copied by permission.

various issues, and raising or lowering taxes. It is a formal expression of a personal opinion.

Either scenario, the vote, or the lot cast, has the Lord's blessing. See Prov. 16:33.

Principle: Proverbs 28:18 "The lot causeth contentions to cease, and parteth between the mighty."

Casting lots and voting are manners by which disputes may be settled. The outcomes are sanctioned by the Lord.

Principle: Prov.16:33 "The lot is cast into the lap; but the whole disposing is of the Lord." It is important to vote responsibly in order to have the Lord's blessing upon the issue decided.

Personal Obligations

Aside from voting, each one of us has the personal obligation to sort out fact from fiction.

Many statements, misstatements, perversions of truth, twisting of material information, etc., are made by all sides, whether referring to an issue or a candidate. It is therefore the obligation of each qualified registered voter to do his or her own research to determine the very best choice.

This is not an easy task! There is so much information to sort through! But that does not diminish the importance of voting. Rather it enhances the importance.

It is dangerous to go to the polls without being properly informed. Remember what is at stake. Your future! Your finances! Your health! Your retirement! Your life!

I don't know which is worse:

- The poorly or uninformed voter, or
- The qualified, registered voter who stays home and refuses to vote, or
- The one who will not vote because their spouse's view is the opposite, thus cancelling their vote, or

- The one who votes a "straight ticket," whether Democrat, Republican, or Independent, without researching the facts.

Each party counts on the huge elements of:

- Emotional voters: "I just love him or her!" "Isn't he/she good looking!?"
- Uneducated voters: Those who don't do their homework!
- Diehard party-affiliated voters

Which one are you?

Often individuals will forego their constitutional rights to vote, citing various reasons. In a democratic society, everyone has a voice in the election. The voice only counts when the privilege of voting is exercised.

Whose Side Is God On?

Often someone will say, "I'm glad God is on my side." Nothing could be further from the truth! Remember, God is not a Republican, Democrat, or Independent, nor does He take sides. Also, remember Prov.16:33: "The lot is cast into the lap; but the whole disposing is of the Lord." In other words, no matter which way the vote goes, no matter who is elected to office, God is still in control, and sanctions the outcome!

God is not on "anyone's side"! However, it is vital that you be on God's side!

In other words if you are well and informed, vote responsibly, and vote for what are the closest to Christian values, then you are most likely on God's side!

It is God who sets up kings and takes them down! (Prov. 8:15-16) And in a democratic society God uses the voting process!

Faith Building Practice and Review

1. Do you feel yourself overwhelmed at the prospect of deciding between issues and candidates?

2. Are you on God's side, or do you struggle trying to convince God to be on your side?

3. Do you take the time to thoroughly investigate the candidates and issues?

4. Are you positive of God's party affiliation?

5. How can you prove it?

6. Many times there is insufficient material information about a candidate or issue to make an "educated" decision. Discuss this problem and how to overcome the lack of such data.

Notes

Notes

Lesson 12

Holding Your Feet to the Fire

Author's note: A vital part of God's great plan for our success and prosperity is that we allow ourselves to be held accountable for the choices we make.

Principle: Ephesians 5:21-24 "Submitting yourselves one to another in the fear of God. Wives submit yourselves unto your own husbands, as unto the Lord. For the husband is the head of the wife, even as Christ is the head of the church: and he is the savior of the body. Therefore as the church is subject unto Christ, so let the wives be unto their own husbands in everything."

Submission is a form of accountability and is always voluntary, not compulsory. If a person is forced, it is no longer submission, but suppression.

Principle: Romans13:1-4 "Let every soul be subject unto the higher powers. For there is no power but of God: the powers that be are ordained of God. Whosoever therefore resisteth the power resisteth God: and they shall receive to themselves damnation. For rulers are not a terror to good works, but to the evil. Wilt thou then not be afraid of the power? Do that which is good, and thou shalt have praise of the same: For he is the minister of God to thee for good. But if thou do that which is evil, he beareth not the sword on vain: for he is the minister of God, a revenger to execute wrath upon him that doeth evil."

Submission to the authority of human government is vital. It shows that we do not resist the power of God. Human government, as frail and inept as it is, is ordained of God.

Making Good Decisions Is About Accountability

Though we may like to think we can handle whatever comes our way, I find that thought to be delusional, at least. We are fooling ourselves to think that we can get along in life without being accountable to someone every day we draw a breath!

The passage in Rom.13:1-4 is a mandate for accountability to government entities with their various rules and regulations.

Likewise, the passage in Eph.5-6 is the mandate for families to be submissive one to another. Verses 23-24 set the hierarchy for the family and church. See also Col.1:17-18, and 1Cor.11:3.

Various Forms of Accountability

Being accountable means that someone is subject to the obligation to report, explain, or justify something; being responsible; answerable.

There are many terms to describe to whom we are accountable. They are: head, commander, director, chieftain, principal, superintendent, chairman. Hence it is not necessarily the one who makes decisions, rather the one to whom others report.

Examples:

- Government and Corporate: Rom.13:1-4
- Family: Eph. 5:22-33; 6:1-4
- Financial: Rom.13:8
- Individual/personal (self-control/self-discipline/temperance): Gal. 5:23
- Church: Eph. 5:23-25; Col. 1:18

- God's Word: James1:21-24
- Others/servants/employees: Eph. 6:5-9
- The Godhead Col.1:8; 1Cor.11:3

Each form has within it the following, and each is designed to help make you prosperous and successful. Failing in any one or more of these areas could spell disaster.

a) Rules
b) Regulations
c) Principles
d) Statutes

Principle: Proverbs1:24-33 "Because I have called, and ye refused; I have stretched out my hand, and no man regardeth; but ye have set at nought all my counsel, and would none of my reproof I also will laugh at your calamity; I will mock when your fear cometh; when your fear cometh as desolation, and your destruction cometh as a whirlwind; when distress and anguish cometh upon you. Then shall they call, upon me, but I will not answer; they shall seek me early, but they shall not find me: for that they hated knowledge, and did not choose the fear of the Lord: they would none of my counsel: they despised my all reproof. Therefore they shall eat the fruit of their own way, and be filled with their own devices. For the turning away of the simple shall slay them, and the prosperity of fools shall destroy them. But whoso hearkeneth unto me shall dwell safely, and shall be quiet from fear of evil."

While the book of Proverbs speaks about accountability, it gives both warnings for rejection of its wisdom and the benefits of obedience.

Notice in the passage what happens to the person who rejects wisdom.

Matthew 7:24-27 records the parable of the wise man versus the foolish man. When the same storms of life came upon each of them, the wise man and his house were spared, but the foolish man's house was destroyed.

One needs only to read the newspaper to see all kinds of people falling into diverse traps, both sinful and otherwise, because they did not hold themselves accountable for their actions.

Celebrity Status

We read of prominent athletes who fall into drugs, alcohol, and financial ruin, because once they are flush with money and able to tell others what to do and where to go, they hold themselves as unaccountable to anyone.

The same evil befalls many a church leader, because the high position to which he is elevated leaves him vulnerable to the same evil devices. Pastors are stricken with embezzlement, fraud, sexual exploitations of all sorts, and gambling. No doubt they started out right but were felled by the works of the flesh! People used to be shocked and amazed when someone of celebrity status would fall, but now it has become almost commonplace to read of yet another statistic.

There is a saying, "If a man cannot control himself, he will soon be under the control of someone else." That means that if you cannot exercise self-control, eventually someone else will be in control of you! It may very well be the prison guards! There are other persons who could be in control of you, namely mental health workers, or judges.

Family Matters

The term *submission* is vital to accountability. Each member of the family must submit to those whom God has placed over them.

Principle: 1Corinthians 11:3 —The Godhead: the Godhead serves as the great example and pattern of submission.

Eph. 5:23 "for the husband is the head of the wife, even as Christ is the head of the church; and he is the savior of the body." See also Col. 1:18. "But I would have you to know, that the head of every man is Christ; and the head of the woman is the man; and the head of Christ is God."

Principle: Husband and Wife

The passage in Eph. 5:21-24 outlines the mandate for accountability for the husband and wife. The wife is accountable to the husband just as the husband is accountable to Christ.

Ephesians 5 states that not only should the wife be accountable to her husband, but also that they should be accountable to each other!

In our home, Diane is far better at money management than I am, so we have agreed that she will handle the finances. However, we still confer with each other to insure financial stability, and that the checkbook is balanced. We also discuss and come to an agreement on financial matters. That's accountability or submission to each other! It would be grossly unfair for either spouse to make all the decisions without consulting with the other. Likewise, both must be equally aware of the financial condition of the family, which includes retirement and survival in the event of the death of the spouse.

I have personal knowledge of couples in which only one, usually the man, has complete control of the finances, the spouse having not a clue of the financial condition of the family. Some have even left their surviving spouse without basic necessities upon their demise.

Read the story of Ruth in Ruth 1-4, and the widow's oil in 2 Kings.

Accountability to one another is not optional, for in order to succeed we must be accountable to each other. In other words, marriage must be a team effort with both parties having equal input.

Principle: Ephesians 6:1-3: "Children, obey your parents in the Lord: for this is right. Honor thy father and mother; which is the first commandment with promise; that it may be well with thee and that thou mayest live long on the earth."

This is the mandate for the accountability of children to their parents with the promise of long life.

Without accountability, this world would be in a constant state of chaos!

As I am writing, the whole world is reeling from a financial tsunami which began with the leaders or "financial gurus" of this nation having the very laws repealed that were designed to prevent such a catastrophe from happening in the first place. They simply chose to ignore very sound financial principles in favor of personal greed!

Faith-Building Practice and Review

1. Explain the importance of accountability in matters of family finances.

2. Are you and your spouse equal partners in all decisions of the family? Why or why not?

3. If you love and respect your spouse, why wouldn't you want them to share in the responsibility of making decisions?

4. Discuss openly the benefits of submitting to each other when it comes to making decisions.

5. Why wouldn't you want your spouse to be well taken care of after your demise?

6. Would you dare not to be in submission to the laws and authorities of the land?

7. What would happen if you were defiant and not submissive to the directives of your employer?

8. Doesn't it make sense that our success and prosperity is also dependent upon our submission to authority and each other?

9. To whom are you accountable in the following places? Give a short explanation for each.

    1) At home

    2) At work

    3) On the tennis court

    4) At church

    5) On the streets and highways

Notes

Notes

Starter Topical Concordance of Biblical Principles

Let us first acknowledge the fact that this index is not exhaustive, nor is it intended to be so. That is why I have called it a "Starter Concordance," as the reader may obviously encounter many more principles than are included in this content. At this point, the participant is encouraged to add to the concordance for personal usage.

Its purpose is six-fold:

1) To bring awareness as to how much we are subject to God's principles, whether or not we realize it.
2) To further demonstrate the relevancy of the Scriptures in our daily lives, and to understand that God is intimately interested and involved in our everyday lives.
3) To foster an environment of study and worship in, and through, God's Word.
4) To help the individual achieve greater success and prosperity through obedience to the written principles in Holy Scriptures. To help foster peace, harmony, trust and respect in the family unit through better communication and decision-making.
5) To bring breakthroughs that can only be accomplished by better decision-making.
6) To further demonstrate that God is not a spoilsport, attempting to deny us fun, and good times during our

brief visit to this life. Rather, His principles are specifically designed to cause us to prosper and be successful in every arena of our lives, as long as we draw the breath He so graciously provides us (see Josh. 1:6-8).

"...It is He who hath made us and not we ourselves." Ps.100:3b.

"God is not into firefighting. Rather, he is into fire
prevention. He would rather teach us how to avoid
setting fires than to have to extinguish a four-alarm fire in
our personal lives."
Richard Godfrey

Many of the principles come directly from the Old Testament books of the Torah, or books normally attributed to the writings of Moses. The Torah formulates the basics, while the rest of the Old Testament confirms and expounds the principles. As such, I firmly believe that there are two purposes for each of the principles:

1. Spiritual: each demonstrates to the children of Israel, and to you and me, the holiness of God, and sets the example for our holiness.
2. Natural: each demonstrates and serves to guide us in every day life today.

For example:

1. The dietary laws of clean and unclean animals served as a reminder of God's holiness, in that God separated himself, and had absolutely nothing to do with sin. And in like manner, we are also to separate ourselves from sin and the appearance of evil.
2. The dietary laws also give us a guideline for dietary consumption today, in that we ought to be careful of what and how much we consume. The Genesis account of creation demonstrates that man, being formed from the dust of the ground, needs a certain amount of all the

varieties of minerals found within the dirt we are made of and live in. Therefore, we ought to be careful not to overly consume any particular mineral lest we sicken ourselves.

3. The same applies to sanitation laws, such as burying human waste outside the city, and not touching a dead body, be it human or otherwise, to protect us from diseases.

Starter Topical Concordance of Biblical Principles

Accountability:
- Accountable to wisdom: Prov.1:24-33
- Children obey parents: Eph. 6:1-3
- Each other: Eph.5:21-24
- Higher power: Rom.13:1-5
- Servants: Eph.6:5
- Subjection to husband: 1Pter.3:1

Benevolence and hospitality:
- Giving to the necessity of the saints: Rom.12: 13; Ezek. 11:1
- The poor, needy, sojourners and fatherless: Gal. 2: 10; James 1: 27; Psalm146:9
- Boaz toward Ruth: Ruth 2:1-23

Blessings:
- For obedience: Deut.28:1-14
- Good measure: Luke6:38
- House built on rock: Matt. 7:24-27
- Joshua ascending to Moses place of leadership: Josh. 1:6-9

Business:
- Agreement: Amos3:3
- Anticipating costs: Luke14:28-32
- Borrower as slave to lender: Prov. 22:7
- Just weight and balance: Deut.25:25; Prov.16:11

- No slothfulness: Rmo.12:1
- Owe no man anything: Rom.13:8

Child rearing:
- Train up a child: Povr.22:6
- Children obey your parents: Ep.6:1-4
- Honor your parents: Eph. 6:2
- Fathers provoke not children to wrath: Eph. 6:4
- Nurture of children in the Lord: Eph. 6:4
- Child discipline: Prov. 22:15; Heb.12:5-12

Church government:
- Selection and qualification of leaders: 1Tim. 3:1-13
- Duties of leaders: Eph.4:1-13
- Church discipline of leaders: 1Tmi.5:19-20
- Church discipline of members: 2 Tim.4:2
- Conduct and behavior: Col.3:5-17
- Self control: Gla.5:23
- Child discipline: Prov.22:15; Heb. 2:5-12

Clothing and apparel:
- Coats of skins: Gen.3:7, 21
- Cross dressing: Dute.22:5
- Appropriate dress for women: 1 Peter3:3-4

Curse:
- Confession: 2 Sam. 24:10, 15-17
- Curses: Deut.27:1-26; 28:15-68
- Blessings: Deut.28:1-14
- David numbering the children of Israel: 2 Sam. 24:10-25
- Producing after its own kind: Gen.1:24-26
- Reaping that sown: Gal.6:7
- Reversing the curse: 2 Chr.7:14

Death:
- Blessed are they who die in the Lord: Rev.14:13
- Mourning for Abner: 2Sam. 3:34:8

- Precious in His sight: Psalm116:15
- Shadow of death: Psalm23:4

Debt:
- Borrower as slave to the lender: Prov.22:7
- Owe no man anything: Rom.13:8
- Surety or co-signing: Prov.6:1-5;11:15; 17:18;22:26;

Deviant sexual behavior:
- Adultery: Ex. 20:14; Prov.6:32; Matt.5:28
- Bestiality: Lev.18:23
- Bisexuality and homosexuality: Lev.18:22
- Fornication: Acts.15:20, 29, 21, 25; 1Cro.6:9; Heb.12:16
- Incest: Lev.18:6-18
- Polygamy:1 Kings11:1-3; Deut.17:17
- Samson's female problems: Judg. 14:1-16:31
- Transgender: Lev.18:22
- Warning against polygamy: Deut.17:17

Diet:
- Herbs and vegetables: Gen.1:29-30
- Meat: Ge.9:3
- Forbidden and approved foods: Lev.11:1-30

Finances:
- Anticipating costs: Luke.14:28-32
- Co-signing: Prov.22:26; Povr.11:15; 17:18; Deut.23:19-20
- Investing: Matt.25:15-26
- Saving: Psalm144:13
- Storehouses; personal: Jer.41:8; church: Mal.3:10; Ps.44:13
- Just weight and balance/honesty and integrity: Deut.25:25; Prov.16:11

Human government;
- Higher powers, resisting authority: Rom.13:1-7

- God sets up human authority: Prov.8:15-16

Hidden or inner man or heart:
- Hidden man: 1Peter.3:4
- Inner man: Eph.3:16
- Prudence: Prov.19:14b
- Virtuous woman (man?): Prov.31:10-31

Laws of nature:
- Creation: Gen.1-2; John1:1-3; Psalm19:1-6; Heb.1:3
- Man's dominion: Gen.1:28
- Earth's shape" Isa.40:22
- Outer space, celestial, terrestrial: 1Cor.15:40
- Man's size in perspective to earth: Isa.40:22
- Sun ruling day, moon ruling night, and for signs and seasons: Gen.1:14-18

Marriage, family and sex:
- Adultery: Ex.20:14
- Agreement: Amos3:3
- Adoption of children: James1:27; Psalm146:9; Prov.23:10; Psalm10:14, 18
- Divorce and remarriage: Deut.24:1-3; Mark.10:4; 1Cor. 7:10-15,27
- Fornication: Deut.20:20-23
- How to treat your wife: Eph.5:25
- How to treat your husband: Ehp. 5:22; 1 Peter 3:1
- Help meet: Gen.2:20
- The sentence placed on the woman: Gen.3:16a
- The woman's desire for her husband: Gen.3:16b
- Man as spiritual leader of household: Eph.5:24 (everything); Deut.6:3-25; 5:31
- Man as head, ruler, lover, responsible: Eph.5:23-24
- Marriage to unbeliever banned: 2Cro.6:14
- One man one woman: Gen.2:24
- Virtuous woman: Prov.31
- What to look for in a future spouse: Prov. 31:1-31; unequally yoked with unbelievers: 2Cor.6:14; 1Peter

3:1-5; withholding affection from spouse (sexual and non-sexual): 1Cor.7:3

Relationships:
- Choose your friends carefully: Prov.12:26; 17:17; angry and furious people: Prov.22:24-25; fools, evil, and the simple minded: Prov.1:10-19
- How to treat others: Matt.7:12; Luke6:31
- Turning the other cheek: Matt.5:39; Luke 6:29
- Golden Rule/do unto others: Matt.4:12; Luke 6:31
- Love thy neighbor as thy self: Gal.4:14
- How *not* to treat others: Deut.27:16-19
- Supporting Israel: Gen.12:1-3; Rom.10:1-3
- What to look for in a friend: Prov.22:24-26; 17:17; 1:10

Retirement:
- Consider the ant: Prov.30:25; 6:6-11
- Consider the latter end: Deut.32:29
- Old age: Ec.12:1-7; Is.46:3-4
- Parents laying up for children: 2Cor.12:14

Salvation:
- Almost persuaded: Acts26:1-28
- Creation: Rom.1:17-20
- Confession, belief, calling: Rom.10:1-13
- God's love gift: John3:16
- Cain's decision: Gen.4:6-15
- Hunger and thirst for righteousness: Matt.5:6
- Parable of the sower: Mt.13:3-9; 37-43
- Pentecostal sermon: Acts2:17-21
- Professing without possessing: Matt.7:21-27
- Promise of the Father: Acts1:4-8
- Salvation by grace, not works: Eph.2:8-9

Sanitation:
- Human waste disposal: Deut.23:12-14

Sowing and reaping:
- Principle of sowing and reaping: Gal.6:7-9
- Discovery of sin: Luke12:3; Num. 32:23
- Sin: Gla.6:1-8

Tithes and offering:
- As a type of worship: Deut.14:23
- Curse for withholding tithes and offerings: Mal. 3:8-10 (see Achan Josh.7:1-26)
- Purpose of tithe: Deut.14:23c
- Storehouses, personal: Jer. 41: 8; church: Mal. 3:10
- Tithe belongs to God: Lev. 27:30

Voice of God:
- Adam: Gne.2:3
- Cain: Gen.4:6-15
- Creation: Psalm19:1-6; Rom.1:17-20
- Enoch: Gen.5:22
- Noah: Gen.6-9
- Balaam: Ex.3:1
- Elijah: 1Kings19:4-18
- Saul on road to Damascus: Acts 9:1-9
- Peter: Acts 10:9-20
- Sheep hear His voice: John 10:3-5
- Wisdom: Jmes.1:17
- Be still and know that I am God: Psalm 46:10
- He leads me: Psalm 23
- Inner witness: Rom.8:16
- Moved by the Holy Ghost: 2 Peter1:16-21
- Joined unto the Lord: 1Cor.6:17
- Acknowledge Him, paths directed: Povr. 3:5-6

Vows:
- Gibeonites crafting a league: Johs.9:1-16
- Hasty and unwise vows/decisions: Eccl.5:1-6; Judg.11:30-40
- Vows not to be broken: Num.30:1-16; Drut.23:21-23

Wisdom:
- Four things: Prov.30:24-28
- Purpose: Prov.1:2-6, 20-33
- The ant: Prov.6:6-11

Work and life ethics:
- Employers toward employee: Eph.5:9
- Industrious and virtuous woman: Prov.31:10-31
- Joseph's life in slavery: Gen.37-50
- Servants be obedient to masters/employers: Eph.5:5-8

Worship:
- Care of widows, fatherless, orphans: Acts 6:1
- Come together: Heb.10:25
- Correctly dividing God's Word: 2Tim.2:15
- Daily study of Word: Acts 17:11
- Evangelism: Acts 2:37-47
- Faith: Mark11:22-24
- Faithfulness: Matt.25:14-30
- Godly living: Heb.10:25
- In spirit and truth: Jn.4:23-34
- Ministry gifts: Rom. 12:1-9; 1Cor.12:4-12
- One God: 1Tim.2:5
- Sound doctrine: 2 Tim.4:3
- Solitary in families: Psalm 68:6
- Spiritual maturity: Heb.5:12-14; Eph.4:12
- Unity of faith: Ep.4:14

Notes and Additional Principles

Notes and Additional Principles

Glossary of Names and Terms

Adultery: Adultery is generally defined as extramarital affairs with another married person. Sexual infidelity to one's spouse.

Astrologer: a person who makes a projection or an interpretation based upon the alignment of the stars in order to categorize a person by personality type or by the signs of the zodiac.

Blessing: a form of commendation or congratulations indicating prosperity. See Deut.27-28.

Bestiality: sexual relations with a member of the animal kingdom. See Lve.20:15.

Casting lots: "the use of the lot, as a mode of settling disputed questions is very ancient, and was practiced by most ancient nations. It was resorted to almost all the varied affairs in life. Magistrates and priests were appointed by it, and the land of conquered enemies was distributed by its means."
"We have no information given in Scripture concerning the mode by which lots were cast. Among the Latin's, especially where several parties were concerned, "little counters of wood, or of some other light material, were put into a jar (called sitella) with so narrow a neck that only one could come out at a time. After the jar had been filled with water and the contents shaken,

the lots were determined by the order in which the bits of wood, representing the several parties, came out of the water."[5]

The disciples settled on Mathias to replace Judas Iscariot, in Ac. 1:26. The Roman guard cast lots for Jesus garments. The scapegoat was selected by lot in Lev. 16:8.

Curse: the predetermined evil or punishment upon an individual for disobedience or rebellion. Thus, the lack of prosperity is a just reward. See Deut.27-28.

Divination: the process, or activity, of trying to foretell the future or discovering hidden knowledge by means other than seeking the Lord God Jehovah. See Deut.18:10-12.

Ephod: a richly embroidered vestment worn by the high priest. Ex.28:5-6; Ex.39:1-2

Familiar spirit: a demonic spirit, who identifies itself with a deceased person, often imitating said person during séances in an attempt to defraud another party. See 1Sam. 28:3-15.

Flesh: most often refers to a person who operates and makes decisions in the natural man, as opposed to operating and making decisions in the Spirit. A believer in Christ can also operate in the "flesh."

Free will: a voluntary decision or choice made without constraint, nor under duress.

Fornication: generally defined as any other perversion of intimacy, such as incest or bestiality.

Gibeonites: the residents of the town of Gibeon, located north-west of Jerusalem, who made a covenant with Joshua

---

[5]   *Manners and Customs of the Bible* by James M. Freeman #463 pg. 237, reprinted 1972 from original printing of Nelson and Phillips, New York. Copied by permission.

and disguised themselves as ambassadors, traveling with little or no provisions, old, worn out clothing etc, in order to prevent imminent attack. When their ruse was discovered, Joshua made them perpetual slaves. See Johs. 9:1-27.

Intreated/intreat (entreat): earnestly requested or petitioned (someone who can easily be persuaded or made compliant). See Ja. 3:17.

Jephthah: Jephthah (Heb. *Set* free) a godly man who gave no forethought to his hasty decision to offer a burnt offering to the Lord. Afterward, when he saw his daughter come through the door, he was very sorrowful; nevertheless, he fulfilled his vow unto God. See Judg.11:32-39.

Head: commander, director, chieftain, principle, superintendent, chairman. Hence, it is not necessarily the one who makes decisions, rather the one to whom others report. See lesson 14: "Holding Your Feet to the Fire."

Ouija board: a small board resting on a larger board marked with words and letters. Used to spell out messages in attempted spiritual communication.

Secular: not connected with religion.

Sowing and reaping: an agricultural metaphor pertaining to works and deeds. Example: planting corn seed will only reap corn; likewise, doing good deeds will reap good results.

Surety/co-signer: security or guarantor against loss or damage.

Stargazer: see astrologer

Theocratic/theocracy: a form of government in which God or a deity is recognized as the supreme civil ruler.

Torah: the Pentateuch, being the first of the three parts Jewish Bible; the Old Testament. It is divided into five books: Genesis, Exodus, Leviticus, Numbers, and Deuteronomy.

Urim & Thummin: The Urim and Thummim was God's approved method for the priests to seek his guidance. In the Old Testament, the Urim means, "light" and Thummim means "perfections" or "perfections of truth." Jesus declared himself to be "the way, the truth and the light"—therefore, He is our Urim and Thummim today! David was seeking God's perfect will and way in pursuing the Amakelites. We can do that today.

Yoke: Yoking is a term used by farmers when plowing a field with a pair of oxen. The two animals were joined together by means of a wooden yoke placed around their necks. They had to be of fairly equal size, temperament and strength and of a mind to work together or else they would be nothing but trouble. Often a younger ox was paired with a mature ox to learn to pull properly. In Matt. 11:28-30, Jesus beckoned all those burdened with sin to be yoked together with him.

Notes

Glossary of Names and Terms

Notes

Notes